MAVERICK LAWYER

Peter Lewi

*To my mother Charlotte Armstrong whose gift for storytelling
gave me the inspiration to write
www.charlottearmstrong.org*

TABLE OF CONTENTS

PROLOGUE

This story is written as a Roman a clef in that it is at least 90% factually accurate with names changed including mine (I am Jake Rodgers) and the names of clients. I have a habit of telling stories about my unusual legal career to anyone who will listen including friends, colleagues and even strangers I meet at restaurants, bars, or my neighborhood Starbucks. Oftentimes these captive listeners will say "Peter, you should write a book" - so I wrote a book. Many lawyers follow a traditional path of joining a large law firm, working their way up through junior associate to senior associate and ultimately becoming a partner. Others become corporate lawyers who are happy to never set foot in a courtroom. For whatever reasons I followed a different path and here is my story.

If you have been a competitive runner, a competitive diver, and a trial lawyer two qualities that are essential are confidence and nerve. Being a bit crazy also helps. I hope you enjoy my story as much as I have enjoyed the journey.

THE ACCIDENT AND THE TRIAL

There is nothing quite as jarring as the loud sound of metal on metal letting you know you have been in an automobile accident. Jake Rodgers was sixteen years old and was driving his father's 1956 Chevy with five male friends on board coming home from watching a movie at the iconic Alex Theatre in Glendale, California. There had been no drinking or drugs—just an innocent Friday night out with his buddies.

The accident occurred at the intersection of Broadway and Brand—the heart of downtown Glendale. Jake was driving south on Brand and had barely entered the intersection when the signal light turned yellow allowing him to legally enter which should have given him time to make it through before the signal changed to red. Before he could make it through, he was broadsided by a car heading east on Broadway.

Upon exiting his car Jake was confronted by the driver of the other car who immediately produced a badge and announced that he was an off-duty Sheriff's Deputy, and that the accident was obviously Jake's fault. When the police arrived, they not surprisingly sided with the Deputy Sheriff and issued Jake a ticket charging him with running a red light. At the designated court appearance date Jake entered a plea of not guilty and a date was set for trial.

All Jake knew about trying a case was what he had learned from watching Perry Mason on television. Perry was a colorful criminal defense attorney created by writer Earl Stanley Gardner. He had a crack investigator, Paul Drake, a colorful secretary, Della Street, and was invariably up against a District Attorney named Hamilton Burger (naturally referred to as Hamburger). When asked by a fan why Perry Mason won every case, actor Raymond Burr who played the part of Perry, famously told her , "But madam, you see only the cases I try on Saturday."

Even as a teenager Jake knew that the show was very unrealistic and created the false impression that to win a case you not only had to establish that the prosecutor had not proven your client guilty beyond a reasonable doubt but had to confront the real culprit in the courtroom and have him confess on the witness stand. Nonetheless Jake found the show entertaining and was a regular viewer.

In preparation for the trial Jake invited the five friends who had been in the car to his house after the end of a school day. Two of the guys who were riding in the back seat remembered nothing until they heard the sound of the collision. Obviously, they would not be helpful witnesses. Tod the third boy in the back along with Ron and Karl who were in front with Jake had vivid recollections totally consistent with Jake's and he asked them to be available to testify. Jake's instincts told him not to overly rehearse his friends but to have them simply tell what happened in their own words. Of course, he did remind them of his very clear version of the events.

Jake then asked himself admittedly with tongue in cheek—"What would Paul Drake (Perry Mason's investigator) do?" This led to a trip to the corner of Broadway and Brand where he sat on a bus bench with paper and pen in hand along with a stopwatch and carefully watched the sequence of the traffic signals in each direction—Green to yellow to red and back to green again. He concluded that consistent with his memory when the light turned yellow enough time was allowed before turning red to allow making it through the intersection before the light going the other way turned green. He therefore concluded that big shot Deputy Sheriff when he saw Jake's light turn yellow in anticipation of his light turning from red to green jumped the gun and thus the collision.

On the day of trial Jake was nervous but surprisingly confident. He felt comfortable in front of a Judge arguing against a law enforcement person at least twice his age. The Deputy Sherriff told his story to the effect that he clearly had a green light, and that Jake ran through a red light, and it was too late to slam on his brakes to avoid hitting Jake.

Jake, in his first cross examination ever, started off by using—what he was to later realize was a fairly common tactic used by experienced trial attorneys—qualifying his opponent as an "expert" on the subject of traffic signals. He asked the Deputy Sheriff if during his law enforcement career, he had ever worked traffic. After an affirmative response he carefully went through the sequence the green, yellow, red-light cycle and then asked a leading question. A leading question occurs when the phrasing of the question suggests the answer the questioner is looking for. A leading question often starts out with "Isn't it true". It is improper to ask a leading question on direct examination and when it happens it is subject to an objection which will usually be sustained. Leading questions on the other hand are allowed on cross examination since it is presumed that you are dealing with a hostile witness. With no knowledge of any of these legal niceties Jake asked: "Isn't it true that the timing and sequence of traffic signals is to allow time for the person who while in an intersection when a light turns yellow time to get through before the red light on the cross street turns green?" The Deputy Sherriff admitted that this is true but of course stuck to his story that Jake's light had turned red before he entered. It became a simple matter of who was telling the truth. They couldn't both be right. Tod, Ron, and Karl performed reasonably well and corroborated Jake's recollection of how the collision happened and both sides rested their cases.

Judges are known for a tendency to rule in favor of police officers in traffic cases for a number of reasons including the fact that the same officers appear before them many times and there is a presumption, although often unfounded, that the alleged violator is in their own self-interest more likely to be untruthful. This case was a little different since the Deputy Sheriff was of course actually a party to the accident and not the officer who issued the citation. To Jake's surprise and delight the Judge while looking straight into the Deputy Sheriff's eyes banged his gavel and pronounced Jake not guilty.

A simple intersection collision not exactly a significant case but Jake's "victory" as a 16-year-old up against an experienced law enforcement officer was to stick to him for many years to come particularly ten years later when he was admitted to the California Bar.

THE ATHLETE

As a young boy Jake loved just about every sport. While growing up there was not much in the way of organized sports until high school. There was a lot of "my neighborhood can beat your neighborhood" games organized by the kids themselves with no parental supervision or interference. Jake had more leadership than athletic skills and despite his downright scrawny body he was always the organizer. At one point he became quarterback for his neighborhood team solely based on the fact that he owned the football.

Upon entering high school Jake gamely tried out for football but after several games "riding pine" as ostensibly the third string quarterback he was politely let off the team. He met a similar fate in basketball where he was 0 for 3 in the requirements of height, speed and jumping ability. These failures relegated Jake to "regular" mandatory gym class the repository for the non-athletes. It was a close call who disliked these classes more – the teachers who otherwise were coaches of the interscholastic teams but were forced into this duty during their off seasons or the students who were forced to take these boring classes which were comprised of "go through the motion" calisthenics or learning to play meaningless games.

Then a funny thing happened – at the end of the class the students were asked to run one lap around the quarter mile track. While not a formal race Jake found himself leading the pack every time by at least 50 yards. Jake thought that maybe he had found a sport , so he showed up at the try outs for the track and field team. He had no comfortable tennis shoes, street shoes were out of the question, so he showed up in bare feet and entered the 1320-yard run (3/4 mile) on a dirt track and to his delight finished far ahead of whoever came in second. The head coach, Vic Francie, approached him. "Where are your shoes young man"? Jake explained that he wasn't sure if would make the team and didn't want to spend money on track shoes for what could only be a one-time use. "Well, you're on the team. You better get yourself a pair of spikes" was coach Francie's response. Jake went on to a successful 3 years on the track team ending up by his senior year as Co-Captain of the varsity team and the best miler in the league. He was recruited to run at Occidental College which at the time was a track and field powerhouse where he continued his running career. After a successful year as a freshman, even winning a gold medal at the Los Angeles Coliseum leading off the two-mile relay in race where Oxy defeated both USC and UCLA, he became somewhat lost in the shuffle as a sophomore when he found himself among many runners who were simply faster than he was leading to some frustrating non-scoring 4th place finishes.

After one 4th place finish Jake walked off the track in disgust and strolled over to the swimming pool which was about 50 yards away from the track where a swimming and diving meet was in progress. The team was headed up by Roy Dennis also the head football coach and who knew a lot more about football than either swimming or diving. Jake approached him, still in his running shorts, and the following exchange took place:

"Coach, I would like to enter the diving competition."
"Do you know how to dive?"
"Of course, I do."
"Have you ever done it in competition?"
"Well actually no".
"Do you know how it works?"
"Not exactly"

Coach Dennis was incredulous but was intrigued enough to explain the process. He explained about the 5 categories of dives: Front, Back, Twisting, Inward and Reverse all spelled out in a Dive Book at a sign-up table next to the pool and that in dual meets there were 6 dives, one mandatory selected by the Judges and the other 5, one from each group which could be selected by each competitor by filling out a card and handing it to the Judges. Jake gamely walked over to the table and poured though the Dive Book which not only listed all the dives in each group but included the degree of difficulty for each. He had to quickly learn the difference between the "official" name of the dive and the lay term commonly used. For example, a jack knife is a front dive in pike position, a swan dive is a front dive in layout position., a cutaway is an inward dive, and a gainer is a reverse dive. There are typically 5 Judges who give a score on a flip card. The highest and lowest scores are thrown out and the average of the other 3 is multiplied by the degree of difficulty. Coach Dennis except for his knowledge about the rules knew virtually nothing else about diving and Jake never had one minute of coaching and was completely self-taught. What a combination!

Jake's interest in diving began when as a young boy he would "show off" at public swimming pools in his home-town of Glendale, California. It just seemed natural to him to spring off a diving board and twist and spin in the air. For whatever reason he had no fear of belly or back flops – he guessed it was that water is very forgiving and thus the risk of serious injury is relatively small. His interest took a big leap forward when his parents while he was in high school put in a swimming pool complete with diving board. At one point he tried sticking the leaf skimming pole into a chain link fence on one side of the pool, attach-ing a string with a rock at the end and throwing it over a branch on a magnolia tree on the opposite side of the pool. This allowed him to adjust the height of the string while keeping close to the board. With the intent of just having some fun Jake had inadvertently created an excel-lent teaching tool. The biggest mistake divers can make is to propel themselves away from the board to avoid hitting it when coming down.

Jake was lucky enough to live across the street from legendary New York Yankee Manager Casey Stengel. A nephew of Casey had become one of Jake's best friends and he spent a lot of time at the Stengel home especially during the off season when Casey and his wife Edna lived at the Essex House on Central Park South. Casey had a swimming pool which of course had a diving board where Jake continued to hone his skills. In the days when the Yankees won both the Pennant and the World Series almost every year imagine Jake's delight when virtually the entire team would pull up in a bus to Casey's home where a big celebration would take place naturally around the swimming pool. Jake would race across the street and had the nerve to put on a diving exhibition in front of some of the best athletes in the world. One year after doing a simple back flip Mickey Mantle said, "Hey kid – how do you do that?" Jake had no idea whether Mickey was serious or just humoring a young boy but of course gave careful instructions as to how to execute this maneuver. Sure enough Mickey got up on the board and did it and from that day forward Jake took credit for teaching this legendary athlete how to do a back flip.

Back to the diving competition – Jake filled out his Dive Card as best he could. He decided to pick dives from each of the 5 groups with a low degree of difficulty because: (a) he couldn't do many of the more difficult dives; and (b) he believed it would be better to get a high score on "easy" dives than to completely blow the harder dives. To be fair he had indeed been on the Occidental 3-meter diving board many times when it was open for recreational diving. There he was in his running shorts rather than the speedo type suits worn by most swimmers and divers when his name was called for his first dive. He climbed the ladder adjusted the fulcrum as far back as it would go to give himself the maximum spring and height above the board and nodded to the judges to indicate he was ready. They nodded back and off he went with his first competitive dive ever which was a front one- and one-half somersault dive in tuck position (this means you are curled up in a ball rather than having your body bent in pike position). What Jake learned quickly was a truly unique aspect about competitive diving (he couldn't think of another sport where this was true) is that there are less than 30 seconds after you enter the water where you don't know whether you did a good dive or blew it but wouldn't know how you scored until your head reached the surface and saw the judges' flip cards. He came to know that your own feeling about how you did (Were your legs together, your toes pointed, did you make a big splash?) was never too far from how you were scored.

To the amazement of Coach Dennis and Tom Campbell who was the other diver on the team he won the competition. Tom, who must have felt very awkward to say the least, was very gracious and welcomed Jake to the team and congratulated him on his win.

Between his junior and senior year at Oxy Jake decided he wanted to be a Newport Beach lifeguard. Although on the swimming team it was just as a diver and altough an OK swimmer he was nowhere near competitive level. At six feet and 140 pounds he certainly did not have a lifeguard build. None of this deterred him. When he was in high school the most popular place to go for Easter week was Balboa Island. Jake went there every year and fell in love with the area, thus the dream to be a lifeguard. There were a few problems – the lifeguard qualification tryouts were on a Sunday morning and he had a Spanish final exam the following Monday. Since he couldn't afford a hotel room he drove to Newport on Saturday, slept in his car in a parking lot at the beach and even studied for the Spanish final using the overhead dome light in his car. The swimming part of the qualification test was a half mile swim in the ocean within a certain time limit.

The Lieutenant in charge dumped about 12 of the aspiring candidates at a time into a spot at the beach which was a half mile from a float where other Lieutenants were waiting with stop watches. Jake found himself uncharacteristically at the back of the pack. As he neared the float the Lieutenants were cheering for him to speed up – he guessed because he was a skinny underdog. He made it in time with only seconds to spare. To top it off he passed his Spanish final the next day. It was a memorable summer sitting in his tower and making his share of rescues. He returned to Newport Beach the next year and enjoyed another summer as a lifeguard. On crowded Sundays of course no one got the day off and thus there were more lifeguards than towers. Sometimes you would get an assignment standing between two towers, where there was a prevailing rip current, holding your yellow rescue buoy, so that you could quickly get to people who were in trouble. Jake was not much for status symbols but he had to admit he liked the prestiege associated with his red trunks and red jacket.

BECOMING A LAWYER

After graduating from Occidental College Jake had a brief fling at graduate school in psychology at the University of California at Berkeley. Finding himself disappointed with the curriclum at the graduate program for psychology he started hanging out with the law students at the UC Law School (Boalt Hall). At Oxy Jake had taken a graduate level psychology course that included administering tests employing projective techniques including the Rorschach Inkblot test to young people incarcerated at the California Youth Authority. When he learned that the first year at Cal Berkeley would be devoted to studying animals in a lab he felt like it was a step backward. Making a seemingly impulsive decision he had a change of heart and decided he would rather be an attorney than a psychologist. Ironically what he had learned about psycholgy as an undergraduate perhaps helped him understand how to listen to the unconcious mind.

Having dropped out of school, he was eligible to be drafted and the best way to fulfill his miliary obligation was to join the California National Guard for six months of active duty. He reported to the Berkeley unit of the National Guard and was shipped off to Ford Ord for Basic Training. His decision to become a lawyer was reinforced by an attorney named Ron Munroe who was a fellow recruit housed at the same barracks as Jake. Ron was already a successful lawyer in Beverly Hills and had taken a break to fulfill his miltary obligation. Ron regaled Jake with stories about his law practice and very much engouraged Jake to enter the profession.

Upon leaving Fort Ord Jake immediately took the Law School Admissions Test (LSAT) and happily achived a high score. Now – where to go to law school? He couldn't afford to go full time without working which left him with night law school programs which were few and far between. He settled on USC because besides having a fine law school it had a night program with the same professors and curriculum as the day program and allowed for full time employment. Because students could only handle 10 units per semester it took four years instead of the usual three. Because Jake was discharged from the National Guard in June it was past the deadline for applying.

Undaunted, Jake drove to USC with his Oxy transcript and LSAT score in hand and marched into the office of Dean Orins Evans. He was able to convince the Dean's secretary to let him meet the Dean who listened to his story about his late attempt to apply being due to his recent departure from the National Guard. Dean Evans looked at the paperwork and said: "Young man – we have had a lot of luck with Oxy graduates and based on this information I will make an exception – Welcome to USC".

It was a grueling four years with the combination of a full time job, classes from 6:00-8:00 p.m. Monday through Friday plus National Guard meetings two Monday nights and one Sunday a month but Jake managed to graduate third in his class. The National Guard meetings were held at an Armory in Glendale. The commanding officer of Jake's unit was Captain Doyle Kolodney who happened to be an attorney. When he learned that Jake was attending night law school he allowed him to use a private room during part of the Sunday meetings to study. Jake was forever grateful for Captain Kolodney's kindness and years later they were opposing counsel in a case which was settled amicably and thus a trial featuring Private Rodgers versus Captain Kolodney was avoided.

One of the toughest parts was Friday night classes when there was a football games scheduled at the Los Angeles Coliseum next door. The band would march by below the window where students were being lectured and the noise from the cheering crowds could be heard. Seventy five started out in Jake's class and only twenty five graduated. It wasn't that fifty flunked out but rather that few could withstand the rigors of a full time job, intensive classes five night a week along with family and other responsibilites. A few years later USC terminated the night Law School program perhaps due to the high attrition rate.

"I solemnly swear that I will support the Constitution of the United States and the Constitution of the State of California, and that I will faithfully discharge the duties of an attorney and counselor at law to the best of my knowledge and ability."

Some heads turned toward Jake because his recital of the oath rose in volume above his colleagues also being sworn in by Judge Tom Murphy at the Superior Court in downtown Los Angeles. He couldn't help himself—his excitement about becoming a lawyer was palpable and he couldn't wait to get started. Imagining himself in a Gene Kelly movie Jake pretty much danced down the courthouse steps. As was the custom his group walked three blocks to the United States District Court to be admitted to the Federal Bar.

In front of Federal Judge David Johnston's Department A of the District Court sat an attractive young blond at a card table with a sign that read: "Federal Indigent Defense Panel—Sign Up". Jake flashed his most charming smile and asked blondie "What's this all about?"

"Well—as you probably know there is no Federal Public Defenders office (This was many years ago)—Bobby Kennedy has set up a Federal Indigent Defense Panel whereby attorneys on a volunteer pro-bono basis represent criminal defendants who can't afford an attorney".

"I'll check back with you after the swearing in ceremony" Jake promised.

This was on a Monday—fast forward to Thursday, Jake's fourth day as a lawyer, and he was standing in Federal Court being assigned to represent Sonny Gardenshire who was charged with two counts of armed bank robbery. This was an arraignment which usually is the first court appearance for a criminal defendant where the charges are formally read, and a plea is entered. The Judge who was well aware of Jake's rookie status explained that he would be taking a brief recess and that the Federal Marshalls would bring Sonny into the courtroom and let Jake interview him in the jury box before entering a plea. Jake brilliantly replied, "Sounds good your Honor". When the Marshalls marched Sonny in, unlocked his ankle shackles and handcuffs, and led him to the jury box Jake thought "This is it – I am really a lawyer".

After a brief continuance to allow Jake time to interview Sonny and review as much evidence as the U.S. Attorney assigned to the case was willing to share, Jake's first case turned out to also be his first plea bargain. The evidence was overwhelming including an amateurish note in Sonny's handwriting: "This is a gun—it's loaded—hand over all your money" and Sonny pretty much acknowledging his guilt. The plea was to one count of unarmed bank robbery. Sonny was sentenced to five years however under then current practices probably got out of prison within 18 months. As much as Jake would have liked to take credit for such a "good deal" it was more a matter of an overly crowed criminal trial calendar resulting in pressure on Federal Judges to have as many dispositions as possible (that's lawyer talk for resolutions without the time and expense of protracted trials). Jake's second case on the Defense Panel on the other hand went all the way to a full-blown jury trial where Jake managed to get an acquittal for a client named Jorge Martinez who was charged with forging Postal Money Orders. At age twenty-six with hair down to his shoulders (not a Hippie—just didn't like haircuts) Jake muddled through the trial objecting to just about everything the prosecutor offered into evidence. To his surprise many of his objections were sustained. There were no emotional hugs after the verdict as is usually seen on television – instead as Jake and Jorge left the courtroom Jorge turned to Jake and curiously said " I'm glad you thought of that acquittal situation" as though Jake had come up with the concept.

When Jake started out it was common practice for any courthouse to start off each day with a Master Calendar which involved a Presiding Judge who would farm out cases for trial, special motions, or other proceedings for any particular case. Master Calendar proceedings were typically in a large courtroom with dozens of attorneys gathered to get their case to the next step in the proceedings. Although seasoned lawyers found Master Calendar to be a boring waste of time Jake thought of it as an opportunity to see how other attorneys much more experienced than he conducted themselves and argued their position on issues large and small. He was fascinated by local "customs"—something not taught in law school and only learned by being "in the trenches". Starting off as a criminal defense attorney he noticed that at first appearances, usually arraignments, attorneys would sometimes ask for a brief continuance to speak to Mr. Green. His curiosity aroused, he asked a veteran, "who the hell is Mr. Green?". The attorney smiled and informed him that it was code for telling the judge the attorney had not yet received a retainer fee. Most judges having once stood in the shoes of practicing attorneys granted the delay to confer with "Mr. Green" knowing that criminal defendants who do not pay up front might never pay their attorney fees.

Since he didn't have a mentor Jake had to learn on his own simple courtroom protocol and customs. Where do you sit at the counsel table? The party with the burden of proof, the plaintiff in a civil case and the prosecutor in a criminal case, sits on the side closest to the jury. Where there is more than one attorney representing a party the lead attorney is known as sitting first chair which is section of their side of the counsel table closest to the center. In most major trials there are at least two attorneys on each side, sometimes even a third who was usually a rookie keeping track of exhibits and learning about life in the courtroom from more senior assocates. This whole "chair" busines was somewhat moot for Jake because he was always first and only chair.

Then there is the no-man's land which is the area between the counsel table and the Judge. The only person allowed there is the bailiff while handing a document or other evidence from one of the attorneys to the judge. Side bars can be requested by either attorney or ordered by the Judge. They are held at the side of the bench farthest from the jury box. They are for the purpose of discussing a matter which should not be heard by the jury until the Judge makes a ruling. If the side bar is going to be lengthy the jury is excused, and the attorneys may adjourn to the Judge's chambers.

Realizing that he couldn't make a living providing pro-bono services Jake transitioned into nickel and dime cases involving possession of marijuana and DUI's. He had rented a small office within the suite of a medium sized law firm in Century City, a sprawling complex just west of Beverly Hills developed on what had been the Twentieth Century Fox Movie Studio lot. While other lawyers in the suite had fancy business clients Jake became known as that guy on the 5th floor who would handle your possession case for $500. His clients included parking lot attendants and trades people such as painters, electricians and drywall contractors working on tenant improvements in the building.

FITZGERALD & RODGERS

After about a year of representing "the common man" Jake had an epiphany created by a luncheon with his old army buddy Ron Munroe. After his first sip of a martini in an upscale eatery on Rodeo Drive Ron asked: "Jake— wouldn't you rather meet clients at a place like this than at the county jail?"

Thus began a quick transition to civil litigation. Having no known marketing skills Jake approached the other lawyers in the suite hoping for some overflow business. Attorney Bill Fitzgerald took a liking to Jake especially when he found out that Jake had graduated third in his USC Law School class. Bill was a fanatic Trojan supporter and made a much bigger deal than Jake about the magic of cardinal and gold. It was in Jake's best interest to go along with the USC connection and besides, he found Bill to be very likable and very smart.

Jake started off doing piecework assignments on an hourly basis but less than six months after starting Bill called him into his office for a meeting and to Jake's surprise and delight offered to make him a Junior Associate and add his name to the door with a firm name of Fitzgerald & Rodgers. He wondered if the name on the door was to entice him to work full time for a very low monthly salary however Bill's enthusiasm about Jake's work seemed genuine and he didn't come across as a manipulative person.

Bill had a general practice which included a very narrow niche specializing in claims against the Federal government based on contract disputes between Bill's clients and various governmental agencies.

Bill introduced Jake to the 3-martini lunch which in his case was not just an expression but a daily ritual. This got Jake into some bad habits which lasted for many years. Jake was too young and naïve to realize that Bill was a full-fledged alcoholic. After eighteen months years working as Bill's junior associate on litigation matters reality set in when Bill collapsed in the office with a burst esophagus a fairly common side effect of cirrhosis of the liver. Eight hours later Bill died after unsuccessful emergency surgery.

So, there was Jake at age 28 with a broken heart—Bill had become very much a father figure as well as a mentor—and a mountain of unresolved pending cases. Surprisingly not one of Bill's clients abandoned Jake for a more experienced attorney—they figured that if Jake was good enough for Bill, he was good enough for them.

John Lennon famously said, "Life is what happens to you when you're making other plans". Jake went a step beyond in that life was happening to him without making any plans.

By hindsight Jake wondered if adding his name to the firm so quickly represented a conscious or unconscious move by Bill based on his deteriorating health and a desire to have a successor to his practice.

In any event Jake had no trouble whatsoever in transitioning from "junior" attorney to trial lawyer of record in the cases he inherited from Bill. Trial lawyers are a special breed thriving on being in the eye of the storm and feeding off the inherently stressful environment of the courtroom.

Jake was grateful for the terrific education he received at USC School of Law. His one complaint looking back was that at the time he attended there was virtually no training as to how to actually try a case in court. They gave you all the tools with courses such as Civil Procedure, Criminal Procedure, Pleading and Evidence but nothing as to how to conduct yourself in the courtroom. Although many law schools had moot court training the closest thing at USC was Appellate Argument where you learned how to write a brief and argue a case up on appeal. For example, less than one hour was spent on Voire Dire (French for "to speak the truth"), which is the procedure for qualifying or disqualifying jurors. There are a certain number of peremptory challenges meaning no reason had to be given, with some exceptions, and unlimited challenges for cause where a bias, prejudice or conflict of interest can be shown. The number of peremptory challenges varies as to civil and criminal cases and in criminal cases the more serious the potential punishment the more peremptory challenges are allowed. In high profile cases with an unlimited budget, professional jury consultants are hired. Some large law firms handling very large cases even stage a mock trial with a mock jury of volunteers to see how the "jury" reacts to the evidence presented. In any event Jake had to learn how to select a jury by the seat of his pants but enjoyed the process.

Many if not most new attorneys go through a mentoring process particularly if they join a large firm. They sit at the counsel table helping the lead attorney with exhibits and otherwise managing the trial but often don't act as lead attorney for at least a year. Jumping right in as Jake did forced him to learn fast but also had its disadvantages some regrettably to the detriment of the client. One of Jake's first civil jury trials after the death of Bill Fitzgerald was a bit of a disaster. He inherited a pending case of Gorman vs. Jack's Machine Shop. Jack McDonald had been a longtime client of Bill's, doing business with his son Jed as Jack's Machine Shop. Jack & Jed had a third partner Robert Gorman who had sued Jack & Jed over a dispute relating to the division of partnership profits over a period of several years. Essentially, he accused Jack of cooking the books and cheating him out of his share of the profits. Gorman was represented by Marvin Diamond an experienced attorney in Pacific Palisades who took Jake to school.

Cases are proven in court with admissible evidence. Offered evidence can be subject to objections the most common of which are irrelevant, incompetent, immaterial and hearsay. Most judges leave it up to the attorneys to make objections to the introduction of evidence by the other side and make a ruling as to whether to sustain or overrule the objection. Some judges will play a more proactive role and disallow evidence even if there is no objection by the attorneys. In the Gorman case the Santa Monica Superior Court judge left objections strictly up to the attorneys and if there was no objection the evidence would be admitted. This led to one of Jake's most serious blunders in trying the case. He basically let Marvin Diamond try a different case than the one that was before the court.

It turned out that Jed was having an affair with Gorman's wife which included some sex acts in an office in the back of the machine shop. Marvin Diamond offered testimony about the affair into evidence and making a horrible rookie mistake Jake failed to make timely objections based on irrelevancy and thus allowed the jury to hear all about the torrid affair. Jake compounded his mistake in the way he handled his expert witness Henry Steinberg. The case was really about forensic accounting and Henry was a CPA who came across as being very arrogant. In qualifying Henry as an expert Jake foolishly asked Henry about his GPA in college. The jury was not impressed with his 4.0 average. Just when one would think it couldn't get any worse Jake took Henry to lunch during the trial and while having a drink with him at the bar in walks the Bailiff with the jury – as the saying goes – not a good optic. At least Jake managed to crowd multiple mistakes into one trial.

Sure enough the jury came in with a verdict in favor of Gorman for the full amount he was claiming. Jake must have had a guardian angel because on a motion he managed to get the verdict set aside based on an assertion that it was based on "passion and prejudice" which in California is an available remedy if the judge believes that the jury based their decision on factors not legitimately related to the case. Jake speculated that the judge on reflection realized that he should have stepped in to deny the admission of the damaging evidence even though Jake did not object.

Gorman appealed and the case was ultimately settled while on appeal. Sometimes it's better to be lucky than smart.

In addition to being "taken to school" by Marvin Diamond in the Jack's Machine Shop case, Jake learned many other lessons from more experienced litigators. One such instance was in a possession of marijuana case during his first year of practice. Two young men who were best friends were charged with what was at the time a serious offence. The judge ordered that they have separate attorneys in case one decided to rat out on the other. Not surprisingly Jake got the one with no money and the friend who had a wealthy father was represented by an experienced Beverly Hills attorney named Josh Williams. Since the two boys had no intention of turning on each other Jake was able to work cooperatively with Josh throughout trial preparation even approaching the Deputy District Attorney together on a plea bargain.

On the day set for trial plea bargaining was ongoing and the Deputy DA asked Josh, Jake, and their clients to step out into the hall. A few minutes later the bailiff came out and announced, "No deal, the judge is ready to start the trial." Jake turned to Josh and in a somewhat panicky voice said, "What are we going to do ? What are we going to do ?" Josh's calm reply stuck with Jake for many years to come – "I don't know about you but I'm just going to go in there and be a lawyer." The lesson was to never count on a settlement or deal and be fully prepared for trial no matter what the circumstances.

If a lawyer tells you he or she has never lost a case, they are either lying or never took on a tough case. Gorman vs Jack's Machine Shop was not the only case Jake lost although thankfully his losses were few and far between. Alco Plating Corporation was another client Jake inherited from Bill Fitzgerald. Glenn Culver, the president, and majority shareholder of Alco, had become a close friend of Bill's and was devastated by his sudden death. Alco's largest client by far was Mattel which employed Alco to perform all the metal plating required in the manufacture of Hot Wheels, an immensely popular toy. Hot Wheels was a genius product in that every child who got hooked was always looking for the next model car to come off the assembly line.

Fortunately, Bill had delegated some Alco matters to Jake. which eased the transition including Jake becoming the Corporate Secretary and a Member of the Board of Directors. Representing Alco had involved routine matters of corporate governance until Glenn approached him with an unusual and challenging assignment which was to represent Alco and eleven other metal platers in an action challenging a provision of the Los Angeles City Business Code which imposed a much higher tax rate on metal platers than on manufactures on the basis that platers were classified as a service. Jake's argument was that metal platers sold products comprised of gold, silver, cadmium, nickel, or whatever other form of metal was required for the plating process.

This was not a class action which requires complex preliminary proceedings to certify a particular group of people as a class but was simply a lawsuit with twelve named plaintiffs. Jake's favorite class in law school was Constitutional Law and he was delighted to finally have a 14th Amendment case involving equal protection of laws. The Los Angeles County Superior Court Judge ruled against Jake and his clients holding that it was reasonable to classify metals platers as a service business. Jakes clients authorized him to appeal and the Appellate Court which upheld the trial court's decision and the California Supreme Court declined to consider a further appeal. To add insult to injury in a published opinion the Appellate Court ridiculed Jake's legal argument and stated that characterizing metal platers as selling a product would be like saying painters are selling paint rather than performing a service.

The words "give up" were not in Jake's vocabulary and fortunately one of his client's had a connection with Tom Bradley. Tom Bradley had a unique and admirable career. The grandson of a slave he rose through the ranks including as an excellent quarter miler at UCLA, followed by long service as a Los Angeles police officer, then law school and a stint in private practice followed by his election as a Los Angeles City Councilman, a position he held when Jake met him. He later went on to be the longest serving Mayor of Los Angeles which honored him with the name Tom Bradley International Terminal as a part of LAX.

The only thing Jake had in common with Bradley besides both being lawyers was their mutual history as track athletes. Tom came through by drafting and getting passed an amendment to the Los Angeles City Business Code accomplishing what Jake had been unable to do in the courts.

Jake's next case out of the many that were pending when Bill died involved a claim on behalf of a contractor against the U.S. Army Corps of Engineers involving the construction of military housing in 29 Palms, California. This case revolved around primarily a very technical issue about lumber specifications. (I know boring—but stick with me).

After the completion of construction, the walls twisted and cracked following a few days of 120-degree heat. More specifically some laminated beams forming a truss system lost their structural integrity and became warped which in turn caused severe cracking throughout the home.

As is often the case during protracted litigation opposing counsel can become quite friendly outside the courtroom while still fighting fiercely during discovery proceedings and at the trial. In this case Jake had gotten to know Alan Greenfield, the attorney for the Corps of Engineers, quite well to the point where they would often have a drink together after a long day of depositions. Far from being a dull civil servant Alan was a colorful character whose passion was betting on the ponies at Hollywood Park. In fact, Jake met him there once and got some valuable handicapping tips.

Jake was a natural storyteller which comes in handy for a trial lawyer. He had a sense of drama and enjoyed goading opposing counsel with what he called his Columbo routine. Some may remember Peter Falk's loveable detective Columbo in the wrinkled raincoat who would come up with a zinger line when least expected.

This all leads up to the following telephone exchange between Jake and Alan:

"Alan, I think you're going to want to settle."

"What are you talking about Jake—you have no case—your contractor screwed up—end of story."

"Well Alan, I've got me a pretty good expert witness on this lumber issue".

"Oh yeah—who is he?"

"His name is Arthur Koehler".

"Who the hell is Arthur Koehler?"

"Well, Alan he's only the guy who solved the Lindbergh kidnapping case" (These were the moments Jake loved best).

"I'm sorry Jake you're going to have to explain that one". (Alan was getting a bit agitated.)

Jake went on to tell the whole story about Bruno Hauptmann who kidnapped and tragically killed the baby of Charles and Ann Morrow Lindbergh at a time when Charles was a famous American hero having been the first one to fly solo across the Atlantic.

It seemed that Hauptmann had climbed to the second story of the Lindbergh home in New Jersey to snatch the baby using a homemade ladder. Koehler was able to track the lumber used to construct the ladder back to the lumber yard it came from and then trace it forward to Hauptmann resulting in the capture and conviction of Hauptmann.

When Jake realized that the lumber issue in his case was critical and in fact probably controlling as to the outcome, he was determined to find the best lumber expert he could find. He called the U.S. Forest Service and after some determined checking got a hold of a helpful person who told him about Koehler who was by then was retired and well into his eighties.

Jake was pleasantly surprised when not only did Koehler answer his call directly but indicated he would be delighted to help. After reviewing all the specifications and other evidence Koehler informed Jake that the Corps of Engineers was clearly at fault for not specifying kiln dried lumber for the laminated beams. We all think that trees die when they are cut down and of course they do however they stay "alive" in a certain sense because they expand and contract depending on their moisture content and the weather. Who hasn't experienced a door that sticks on a rainy day? As Koehler explained to Jake because the lumber in question had not been kiln dried it was "wet" and not suitable for desert heat. For that reason, when the 120-degree weather hit the beams dried out, contracted, and caused the damages that were the subject of Jake's claim against the Corps of Engineers.

Sure enough, on Alan's recommendation the Corps settled on a basis very favorable to Jake's client. The irony that the U.S. Forest Service had at least indirectly helped prove a claim against the U.S. Army Corps of Engineers did not escape Jake.

When trial lawyers finish a trial or settle a case there is always the next one waiting in the wings. Jake's next case was much more challenging than the lumber case he had just finished.

Again, one of the cases from the legacy of Bill Fitzgerald—this was a very large "rock claim" as they have come to be called. Once more a military housing project, this one at Mountain Home Air Force Base just outside of Boise, Idaho. The case had been initiated by Bill and had become quite stale by the time Jake took over having been pending for several years. Jake wondered somewhat guiltily if the long delay was in some way attributable to Bill's alcoholism and that perhaps he should have been tending to the matter instead of drinking so many martinis. This was a case of the pot calling the kettle black since Jake had become no slouch in the drinking department.

Having become attorney of record in the case it was time for an introduction to Jerry McCarthy the Air Force attorney assigned to defend the claim of Jake's client. Jerry took being Irish seriously and speaking of alcohol he could put anyone under the table. During the next year that the litigation dragged on Jake got to know Jerry very well since they met many times at many places—Boise, Los Angeles, and San Francisco to name a few. Jake seemed destined to become involved with heavy drinkers. Jake and Jerry got to the point where they would travel together to various locations to take depositions of many witnesses who had scattered to the winds due to the passage of time. In those days drinks on airplanes were served in miniature bottles that fit in the palm of a hand. At one point Jerry demonstrated a technique whereby after ostensibly emptying the small bottle into a glass, by gripping it tightly the warmth of your hand would cause condensation on the inside of the bottle resulting in a few extra drops of alcohol. Now that's a serious drinker!

A bit about the case—When Jake's client, Mountain Home Contractors. began excavation to pour foundations for the 300 homes scheduled to be built the earthmoving subcontractor encountered solid basalt rock—in fact over 100,000 cubic yards of it. The best Caterpillar had to offer cannot excavate solid rock and thus it became necessary to blast the rock using dynamite, an operation much more complicated and expensive than conventional excavation. The Air Force contended that encountering subsurface rock was a risk the contractor took, and they should have found out about it during their due diligence leading up to their successful competitive bid. Jake of course took the opposite view and argued that the test borings provided by the Air Force as a part of the bid package were inadequate.

The person who should have been Jake's star witness turned out to be a disaster. Jimmy Martin had been the project manager and despite the fact that he was the single person with the most direct knowledge of the day-to-day operations he turned out to be very problematic and not as cooperative as Jake would have expected. Although nominally friendly to Jake there was a sense that Jimmy wasn't going to let a young punk lawyer about 30 years his junior tell him what to do. Instead of helping to prove the claim against the Air Force he just went through the motions reluctantly and more importantly had kept horrible records during construction.

Over time Jake figured out why Jimmy was so unenthusiastic about helping with the case. Mountain Home Contractors was comprised of three partners and Jimmy as the guy running the job felt that he should have been made a partner. Since he was a "mere employee" he did not stand to gain financially from the case and there was some residual bad blood between Jimmy and the partners. His hostile attitude can best be exemplified by an exchange that took place at the beginning of his deposition taken by Jerry McCarthy. Jerry started off with the standard request at the beginning of any deposition right after the witness is sworn in:

"Please state your full name for the record."

Jake watched Jerry's eyes roll back in his head when Jimmy responded: "Will you please rephrase the question?" Jerry knew he was in for a long afternoon and Jake wondered how he was going to overcome the impact of Jimmy's antipathy toward his client. Besides the issue as to which party had taken the risk of encountering so much solid rock there were substantial issues as to the quantity of rock removed and the cost of excavation and removal.

Jimmy was such a poor witness that had the matter gone to trial Jake would have had a dilemma in that it would look very strange if he didn't call Jimmy to the witness stand. Even this move would have done no good since Jerry undoubtedly would call him to the stand. Normally under such circumstances he would be called as a "hostile witness" so that he could be asked leading questions as though he were being cross examined. In this case Jimmy stood to be in effect a witness for the Air Force.

One of the consequences of cases getting old is that key witnesses can disappear. It turned out that Jimmy Martin notwithstanding the absolute critical witness in the case was a guy named Joe Flint. Joe was what is called in the industry a "powder monkey" which is a rather inelegant term used to describe a person with enough expertise in explosives (usually dynamite) to supervise large excavation projects. Powder monkeys were often itinerant since jobs requiring their skills (dams, bridges, tunnels, etc.) were few and far between. They had to travel where the action was. As far as anyone could tell Joe had disappeared from the face of the earth. At the time Bill died he had pretty much given up on finding Joe which perhaps was one of the reasons that the case was stalled. Jerry McCarthy couldn't find him either but was not too concerned because the burden of proof was on Jake's client and the passage of time was favoring the Air Force.

Jake being the new kid on the case was determined to find this elusive "smoking gun" (pardon the pun) witness. Big law firms had private investigators working for them but Jake being a solo practitioner was his own detective. Besides the issue of saving money, he discovered that detective work was his favorite part of litigation and seemed to come naturally.

On every trip to Boise he asked everyone he ran into who was remotely connected with the job if they had any idea of whatever happened to Joe Flint. He frequented bars where construction workers were known to hang out. Finally, he came across a clue from a guy named Fergie a concrete subcontractor who bragged about being on his 4th martini. Asked if he knew Joe Flint he replied: "Hell yes known him for years—Our paths have passed many times. I often come on a job to pour concrete right after he has blown up a lot of rock.". "Any idea where he is now?" asked Jake hopefully. "Last I heard he was holed up in some trailer park in Orofino waiting for his next job. Probably snowing like hell up there about now"

Bingo—that was all Jake needed. First, he had to figure out where Orofino was. Turned out to be a very small town in Idaho about 250 miles north of Boise. Jake immediately rented a car and headed north. Orofino is a picturesque town on the banks of the Clearwater River with a population of around 3,000. It made sense that Joe Flint might be there since the Dworshak Dam was nearby perhaps in need of a "powder monkey" with Joe's skills for some serious blasting of rock. Fergie wasn't kidding about the snow—it was about three feet deep on Jake's arrival in town.

On the main drag, actually the only street, Jake spotted a General Store which looked like it could be a hangout for the local residents. Sure enough the proprietor not only knew Joe but told him which trailer he lived in at an RV Park up the road. Jake knocked on the trailer door with great anticipation. A grizzled Joe Flint answered and as soon as Jake told Joe who he was and why he was there Jake knew he had found his man.

Joe not only remembered everything about the rock blasting operation at Mountain Home Air Force Base but was anxious to help since he felt strongly that Jake's client had been screwed by the Air Force. A blasting foreman of Joe's experience had to be a kind of a de-facto geologist. You can't just start setting off huge dynamite explosions without knowing a lot about rock formations below the surface of the ground.

Joe was able to totally refute the government's argument that the contractor should have known about the rock from the test borings supplied with the bid package. It turned out that there was a huge concentration of solid basalt beneath the surface at the job site, but it was very wavy with dips some of which went far below the surface. By a sheer fluke, the places where most of borings were made happened to be consistent with the dips and thus many of the borings did not hit any rock. Joe also knew a lot about the quantity of rock that had to be blasted and removed and how to prove it. In those days record keeping was very haphazard—no hard drives, cloud storage or anything of the sort. People relied more on plain old paper files and although Jimmy had been extremely remiss, Joe had kept meticulous records which he still had locked away in this trailer.

Once more Jake was able to make one of his favorite calls.

"Jerry—I think you are going to want to settle".

"What are you talking about—you can't prove your case."

"I found Joe Flint."

"What do you mean you found him—where is he? We have been looking for him for 2 years".

"It's very nice here in Orofino—I have his statement and you're not going to like it".

This revelation naturally led to the immediate noticing of Joe's deposition by Jerry. Joe held up extremely well under Jerry's vigorous cross examination with both testimony and supporting documentation. When Jerry pressed him on proof of the quantity of rock that had to be blasted and removed Joe produced detailed records including truck load counts and the capacity of each truck.

The production of Joe as a witness after the litigation had been languishing for years was a wakeup call for Jerry who decided that his traveling martini road show with Jake had to cease in favor of serious consideration of the merits of the claim. The result was a $630,000 check from the Air Force to Mountain Home Contractors in full settlement.

No sooner had Jake successfully settled the "rock claim" when Mountain Home Contractors presented him with another dispute left over from the Bill Fitzgerald era. This once again involved military housing constructed for the Unites States Air Force and an esoteric narrow nuance having to do with the interpretation of contracts with Federal agencies. Without going into details which would be quite boring except for the people directly involved, suffice it to say that after protracted litigation the case ended up in the United States Court of Claims in Washington D.C. The case did not actually involve a lot of money (less than $100,000) and Jake felt that the U.S. Attorney's office had somewhat unfairly picked his client's claim as a test case to get a ruling from the Court of Claims as to an unsettled area of law on the theory that if they lost it would not cost the government too much money. Jake's client to their credit felt strongly enough about their position to finance the case as far as they had to go to get a decision. The U.S attorney that Jake dealt with was Robert Donlan however the lead attorney on the pleadings was William Ruckelshaus who was to become famous several years later for resigning along with his boss Elliot Richardson rather than obey President Nixon's order to fire Archibald Cox who was investigating the Watergate matter in what became known as the "Saturday Night Massacre".

When the day arrived for oral argument before the Court of Claims one can only imagine the state of Jake's nerves as at the ripe old age of 32 he stood at the podium before seven justices knowing that he had to be prepared to answer any questions they might ask about his client's position. The bench in most higher courts is higher than trial court benches and the Justices look down at the attorneys.

Reading the tea leaves based on the questions that are asked can be difficult because sometimes a question that seems negative to your position is in fact a bit of "devil's advocacy" from a Justice who is trying to gain support for the direction in which he is leaning. A test case before seven

Justices would virtually never be decided from the bench and as is normal the matter was taken under submission.

Jake and Bob Donovan had become friendly adversaries during the litigation and after the conclusion of oral argument Bob invited Jake to join him for a drink. Bob who of course knew Washington much better than Jake selected a bar downstairs in a nearby hotel. Jake did not pay much attention to the name of the hotel however three years later he realized that he had enjoyed a martini at The Watergate.

Martinis seem to be a recurring theme throughout Jake's career. What is the allure of a martini? First of all, Jake was a purest—a martini is supposed to be just gin with or without vermouth and definitely with an olive. Jake could put up with the switch by many from gin to vodka but then along came the cosmopolitan—such sacrilege—ruining a good vodka with cranberry juice. What's that all about? This was soon followed by various other tutti-frutti variations—blasphemy. On the rocks doesn't work either—must be straight up in the elegant seductive glass—frosty on the outside—shaped like a beautiful woman with the olive as a finishing touch of artistry. Nostalgia was part of it—the old classic movies. Can you imagine Fred Astaire drinking a beer? Humphrey Bogart sipping a glass of wine in Casablanca? Then of course there was shaken not stirred as favored by James Bond.

To the gratification of Jake and his client the decision rendered several weeks later was 7–0 in favor of Mountain Home Contractors in a case that established new precedent as to the issue before the court.

Shortly after receiving the decision, Jake had a celebratory dinner with Robert Dupont the managing partner of

Mountain Home Contractors. After a couple of martinis and some self-congratulatory exchanges about the victory in the Court of Claims, Robert caught Jake off guard.

"I have an interesting assignment for you having nothing to do with construction or litigation". Jake, always eager for a new challenge patiently waited for the details.

It turned out that Robert's passion which was rapidly changing from a hobby to a business was raising Appaloosa racehorses. He was on the Board of Directors of Cal Western Appaloosa an organization dedicated to the advancement of the breed.

"I would like you to write and get passed a law legalizing pari mutuel wagering on Appaloosa horses at County Fairs here in California."

"Funny, I don't remember being elected to the California legislature".

Jake's relationship with Robert had become much more than attorney—client and their friendship made Jake comfortable with his wise-ass reply.

Over dinner, coffee, and brandy Robert expounded on California Horse Racing Law 101. The California Horse Racing Act is a part of the Business and Professions Code and covers all aspects of racing including what breeds could race and where they could race. At the time there were only three breeds that could legally race—thoroughbreds, quarter horses and standardbreds (who engaged in harness racing).

As to Jake not being an elected legislator Robert was ahead of him and had already lined up Robert Moretti an assemblyman from Van Nuys where one of the other members of the board lived. Moretti knew nothing whatsoever about horse racing but was willing to be the "author' of whatever bill Cal Western wanted to introduce. Moretti was a wonderful person who later became the Speaker of the California Assembly. Elected to the assembly at age 30 he tragically died before his time at age 48.

Jake had heard of Appaloosa horses but only knew that they had spots usually on their rear flank and that Chief Joseph the head of the Nez Perce tribe was usually depicted on the back of an appaloosa.

He quickly learned of their four distinctive characteristics which besides the coat pattern included mottled skin around the lips and nose, stripped hooves and white sclera which is the part of the eyes surrounding the iris. Appaloosa racehorses are bred to compete in distances longer than a quarter horse and shorter than a thoroughbred. Robert gave Jake a business size card showing the 4 traits including pictures which came in handy when almost everyone he dealt with in the course of his assignment asked: "What the hell is an appaloosa horse?"

The law Jake wrote was one sentence long and read:

"Any County Fair that conducts a program of horse racing with pari-mutuel wagering <u>may</u> include one appaloosa race per day provided that sufficient appaloosa horses are available".

Someone much more knowledgeable than Jake about horse racing politics told him to make the law permissive (i.e., may) and if his clients proved that appaloosa horse racing was successful (i.e., made a lot of money for the state of California) go back the next year and change *may* to *shall*.

Jake ended up testifying 6 times in Sacramento, 3 times in the Assembly and 3 times in the Senate. Bob Moretti and Jake had their drill down. Moretti would step up to the podium with Jake sitting behind him in the first row of the hearing room. As soon as an assemblyman or senator asked a question about appaloosas Moretti would motion Jake to join him at the podium. Compared to trying a case in court Jake found these proceedings to be stress free and even enjoyable. There didn't seem to be much opposition until one day after the last hearing Jake got an urgent call from Moretti.

"Reagan is going to veto the bill."

"What do you mean—why would he be opposed to it."

Jake's naivete was showing. Reagan was a thorough-bred man. Racing opportunities were zealously guarded by each of the breeds. The addition of an appaloosa race to the card meant one less thoroughbred race. After letting Jake take center stage during the hearings Moretti demonstrated his political savvy and overcame the veto threat and not only got the bill passed and signed but with Jake's help got the change from permissive (may) to mandatory (shall) enacted the following year.

CAMDEN INTERNATIONAL

Legal careers can take many twists and turns. Out of the blue, Jake got a call from Vic Roberts. Vic had been Jake's boss at an aerospace company where Jake had worked while attending night law school at USC. By the time of his call to Jake, Vic had become General Counsel for Camden International Corporation a public company on the American Stock Exchange.

Vic said he had heard about Jake's success handling claims against the government and wanted to know if Jake would be interested in representing Charlie Freiberg, a friend of Vic's, in a claim against the U.S. Navy. Jake not only handled the case but took it to trial in Washington D.C. and recovered 100% of the amount Charlie was claiming for performing extra work on a Navy job.

Charlie naturally reported back to Vic about the excellent job Jake had done. When Vic called to thank and congratulate Jake he asked if Jake could get a transcript of the trial. Normally there is no transcript unless there is an appeal but when Jake contacted the court reporter, she was happy to prepare a transcript for a few hundred dollars. It was out of character for Jake not to ask Vic why he wanted the transcript, but his instincts told him to just get it.

A few days after receipt of the transcript Vic invited Jake to meet him for lunch at the Polo Lounge at the Beverly Hills Hotel. Jake was impressed—the Polo Lounge was a legendary spot famous for business lunches often involving the rich and famous of the Hollywood\Beverly Hills crowd.

You don't become General Counsel for a publicly traded company without some pretty good negotiating skills and Vic was no exception. After some routine "let's get caught up" exchanges and into their second martini Vic got down to business.

"Have you ever thought about getting out of the private practice grind including always looking for your next case and the hassle of billing clients and paying overhead?"

Jake, no slouch at negotiating himself, merely replied: "I'm listening".

Vic went into a long dissertation about how Camden was tired of paying outside counsel comprised of large firms that tended to be billing machines and how he thought it could be a win-win for Jake to come on board with a title of Assistant General Counsel with the responsibility of handling all litigation for Camden and its many wholly owned subsidiaries.

After laying out a detailed offer covering salary, stock options and other benefits Jake told him he was very flattered and needed a few days to think about it. In reality Jake had made up his mind before the second olive in the second martini had made its way to his stomach. He had loved his private practice but Vic's timing was uncanny and Jake was ready for a change. His wife Laurie readily endorsed his decision since she thought the corporate world might be less stressful than the responsibility of running an office.

The transition was remarkably quick. The other attorneys in the Century City suite were happy to let Jake cancel the rest of his lease term and take over as many of his clients as they could. Thus, early on a Monday morning Jake joined corporate America something he never dreamed would happen. He immediately took over a number of Camden cases involving many of its subsidiaries.

Vic summoned Jake into his office and asked him to file a lawsuit on behalf of Fairbanks Helicopter Company a Camden company headquartered in Alaska which had been stiffed to the tune of $500,000 for allegedly overbilling Tiger Construction a contractor in Washington state on a job involving providing helicopter services to help string power lines across the Washington\Idaho border. Stringing a sock line as it is called is a delicate process requiring tremendous skill on the part of the pilot. In this case there were six pilots working for Fairbanks all seasoned veterans of the war in Vietnam. Imagine threading a needle by remote control by hovering and moving carefully while aiming a power line being dragged to the right spot on a tower.

Such jobs are billed on what is called a wet rate which means an all-inclusive hourly rate covering the helicopter, the pilot, fuel, insurance, and all other expenses plus a reasonable profit. The hourly rate at the time of the job averaged $1,250. Customarily billable hours in the industry means actual hours in the air which are measured by a device called a Hobbs meter. Tiger was claiming that the Hobbs meters were rigged and were showing hours far more than the actual hours in the air and thus the refusal to pay the Fairbanks invoices.

Jake's first task was to determine the proper jurisdiction and venue for the case. It turned out to be the United States District Court for the Eastern District of Washington which is in Spokane. Since Jake was not a member of the Federal Bar in Washington, he had to be admitted pro hac vici which is a fancy Latin term meaning "for this occasion only". It is a simple matter of finding a local attorney to make a motion stating that you are a member in good standing of the California bar and have a legitimate need to try a case in a different jurisdiction.

Opposing counsel in the Fairbanks v. Tiger case was Owen Stewart one of the top trial lawyers in Washington state who had his own firm in downtown Seattle. Over the next 12 months Jake and Owen got to know each other quite well and developed mutual professional respect. There were many depositions mostly in the Seattle area or in Fairbanks. Both parties dug their heels in and the odds for a settlement were pretty slim. Finally, about two weeks before the scheduled trial date Owen called Jake with a settlement offer of $250,000. Jake knew he didn't have a slam dunk case and the offer was a respectable starting point given the issues in the case. Jake immediately set up a meeting with Vic to discuss the offer.

Vic was what litigators describe as an armchair lawyer. While sitting in his leather chair behind a mahogany desk he was very "tough", but God forbid that he would ever set foot in a courtroom himself. He not only rejected the offer but wouldn't authorize Jake to make a counteroffer and basically said "Go to trial. That's why I hired you".

Jake practically apologized to Owen for not even countering and in effect said, "see you in court". There is a moment in court proceedings known as "Answering Ready". After months and often years of pre-trial proceedings including depositions, other forms of discovery, motions, continuances, and settlement conferences the trial date finally is at hand and the Judge calls the case and asks counsel to state their appearances. Traditionally the plaintiff's attorney goes first.

"Good morning your honor. Jake Rodgers ready for the Plaintiff."

No matter what any lawyer tells you "Answering Ready" brings a lump in the throat and mixed emotions. Even if you feel you are thoroughly prepared there is a feeling of anxiety based on fear of the unknown coupled with relief that the trial is finally going to begin. Most often trials take place within the jurisdiction of at least one of the two lead attorneys trying the case. Spokane is about 300 miles from Seattle and 1200 miles from Los Angeles. Thus, both Owen and Jake and their respective entourages, including some of the witnesses, stayed in a Spokane hotel - in this case the same hotel which was in a twelve-story building featuring a cocktail lounge on the top floor. This created an unusual dynamic during the week-long trial when each evening Owen and Jake would be holed up with their respective clients and the witnesses for the next day across the room from each other. Occasionally Owen and Jake would pass each other on the way to the rest room and nod an awkward but friendly hello.

Attorneys never know where ideas may come from in handling a particular case. While in law school and early in Jake's career one of the best-known attorneys in California was Melvin Belli who became known as the King of Torts for his flamboyant style and sense of theatrics in the courtroom. When someone accused Belli of being an ambulance chaser he replied: "You're wrong—I get there before the ambulance."

He was particularly known for producing dramatic demonstrative physical evidence. In a well-known case he represented a plaintiff who had lost an arm in a water-skiing accident. Each day he walked into the courtroom with an oblong object wrapped in brown butcher paper. The jury and even opposing counsel assumed in horror that it was the severed limb. Instead, Belli called an expert witness and tore off the wrapping paper to reveal a prosthetic arm which the expert testified Belli's client would have to wear for the rest of her life. The jury came in with a very substantial award of damages It was difficult to know how much Belli's theatrics contributed to the result but this tactic had become his trademark.

Even though this was to be a bench trial without a jury, Jake felt he needed to take a page out of Belli's play book and in some dramatic way convince the judge that the Hobbs meters were not rigged. After presenting all the usual evidence and testimony that might be expected in a trial of this sort Jake adopted an unusual strategy of making a motion which he knew would undoubtedly be denied while having a Plan "B" ready. "Your Honor—I would like to move that your honor, opposing counsel, the court clerk and the court reporter take a helicopter ride this afternoon".

Jake had to smile based on the startled look on Owen's face.

"You're going to have to explain the basis of your motion Counsel".

"Well your honor we want to demonstrate exactly how these Hobbs meters work and show the court that they definitely measure only hours in the air and simply are not set up to measure hours on the ground thus establishing that my client's invoices were in no way padded."

"That's a very interesting motion Counsel but we're not getting in any helicopter—please call your next witness if you have one".

"I would like to request a brief recess while I bring in my next exhibit" replied Jake as he prepared to launch Plan B.

"We will take a 15-minute recess" ordered the Judge giving Jake a look that said, "This better be good".

About two months before the scheduled trial date Jake had a meeting in Fairbanks with Norm Johnston the CEO of the helicopter company, Rick Pratt the chief pilot and Joe Richardson the head mechanic. He floated the idea of fabricating a large mockup representing the critical portions of the helicopters used on the Tiger job to demonstrate exactly how the Hobbs meters were calibrated to only keep track of hours in the air and not engine warm up or warm down time as the defense was claiming. Norm was very skeptical, but Rick and Joe were intrigued by the concept and totally on board for giving it a shot.

It turned out to be remarkably simple. The time in the air as measured by a Hobbs meter activated by the collective which is the stick next to the pilot which when lifted or lowered controls the torque of the spinning propeller. When the torque reaches the level needed for lift off the meter activates and conversely when the torque is lowered to the point where the helicopter touches down the meter stops.

The exhibit was a simulation created by Rick and Joe of essentially like a part of the helicopter and was quite large. For dramatic effect Jake asked them to include the pilot's seat along with the collective, a Hobbs meter and other components sufficient to demonstrate how the system worked.

Joe testified that the mocked-up exhibit was configured exactly like the helicopters used on the job. He was able to sit in the pilot's seat and manipulate the collective to show at what point the meter engaged or disengaged which he testified correlated with the actual flight hours. The Judge was fascinated and stepped down from the bench, sat in the pilot's seat and operated the collective to see for himself how the meters worked.

When Owen vigorously challenged the notion that the simulation accurately reflected the conditions in the field, Jake was ready for him. He offered a parade of witnesses comprised of the veteran pilots who uniformly testified that the mockup accurately reflected conditions in the field. Having flown under enemy fire in Vietnam there was no way they were going to be intimidated by any attorney even under the most rigorous cross examination. When Owen asked "isn't it true" type leading questions the pilots reinforced the testimony they had given on direct examination.

The Judge took the case under submission and Jake had to return to Los Angeles and nervously await the written opinion. When it arrived in the mail about a week later, he was elated to see that the Judge had awarded the full amount claimed plus interest, court costs and attorney's fees. He was convinced that the exhibit made the difference and silently thanked Melvin Belli.

INDIA

Although Vic congratulated Jake for the result obtained in the Fairbanks case, within the company hierarchy he took a lot of the credit for being so "tough" and insisting that the case go to trial. He nonetheless had come to respect Jake's tenacity and called him to his office with an interesting new assignment.

"We have a large Sikorsky S-58T helicopter stuck in Madras, India (now Chennai) and I would like you to go over there and get it." Jake was a bit confused since he was an attorney not a pilot, but Vic quickly explained.

Something that Vic failed to mention at that first lunch at the Polo Lounge was that Camden was going into a downward economic spiral. It had grown as a conglomerate in the 1960's when acquisition sprees were fairly common. A parent company would buy up subsidiaries willy nilly often without much due diligence. The methods of acquisition included everything from hostile take overs sometimes involving a proxy fight, purchase of companies in financial distress and leveraged buy outs (LBO's).

Although Jake felt he had become a good attorney, when it came to public companies, the stock market and corporate finance he was woefully ignorant. He barely knew how to read a balance sheet. He remembered when a colleague explained LBO's in a colorful but easy to understand way.

"It's like buying a cow and paying for the cow with the milk it produces".

Banks were eager to loan and many would help finance LBO's with little or no down payment relying on irrationally overly optimistic projections of future sales and revenue.

By the time Jake joined Camden an intense program of divesting and selling off unprofitable companies had begun. The company was suffering from a huge cash squeeze and was unable to pay its debts on a timely basis. Unbeknownst to Jake this was a major reason for hiring him at a salary much lower than the huge fees being charged by outside law firms that were well known for being billing machines.

It was also the reason for the trip to India. The Sikorsky had been used in connection with what had been a lucrative contract with the Indian government to help in a project to map previously unmapped property far outside any of the major cities. The contract ended and Camden was left with large unpaid bills for many services including hanger rental, mechanics, local taxes, etc. A series of liens had been filed against the helicopter by unpaid creditors including governmental agencies. The liens prevented the helicopter from leaving India air space. Jake's assignment was to negotiate with the creditors on a bare bones budget to get huge discounts of the amounts owed and get the liens released so that the Sikorsky could be moved to where it could be put to use profitably in Singapore and Indonesia.

Madras is approximately 9,000 miles from Los Angeles and getting there involves a grueling flight of more than 24 hours. Jake had booked a room at the historic Connemara Hotel in the heart of Madras. After getting settled in after the long flight Jake took a much-needed walk on the streets of Madras. The first time one sets foot on Indian soil there is a total shock to the system and a bombardment of the senses with sights, sounds, colors, and smells never before experienced. Any part of Western Europe seems like the town next door compared to India which is much more "foreign" to an American. Layered onto the dramatic cultural differences is the horrific sight of thousands of beggars crowding the streets. Many of them were young children often with visible deformities. In his short one week stay in Madras Jake learned the sad truth. Begging was much more than it appeared to be on the surface. First of all, there were gangs in control of many of the beggars who skimmed off the top some of the meager contributions from tourists. Secondly some of the maiming and disfiguring was either self-inflected or actually inflicted by the "bosses" because it "increased earnings". Something that remained etched in Jake's mind forever was the sight of a beautiful young lady with gorgeous big eyes with no legs kneeling on a skateboard on her stumps and propelling herself with her arms pushing along the pavement. She was not actively begging and greeted Jake with a smile. It was heartbreaking. At one point Jake was approached by a beggar dressed slightly better than the others who offered his services to walk with Jake and fend off the other "lower level" beggars. It seems that any group of people even beggars inherently end up with a hierarchical structure.

Jake was an inveterate runner starting off almost every day with a 3–5-mile jog. He particularly enjoyed running in foreign countries and found that jogging whether it be in the center of town or in the countryside was a terrific form of sightseeing. While jogging one is closer to the action and experienced sights, sounds and smells which would be missed in a car or bus. On that first morning in Madras Jake walked out the front entrance of the Connemara hotel to begin his usual run. He found himself weaving in and out of many poverty-stricken people including beggars and for the first time in all his travels felt uncomfortable in his $30 shorts and $100 running shoes. He ceased running for the rest of his stay and made do with long walks in street clothing.

During his representation of Camden, Jake had come to very much like and appreciate helicopter pilots. They were a special breed who worked hard and played hard. They enjoyed their cocktails but as far as he knew every pilot he had met was scrupulous about more than abiding by the FAA 10 hour "bottle to throttle" rule meaning no consumption of any alcohol whatsoever less than 10 hours before liftoff. One evening at the Connemara. Jake ran into a group of 5 Canadian helicopter pilots who obviously had no flights scheduled the next day. They welcomed Jake into their festivities and had a memorable evening of drinking and storytelling. One of them with a twinkle in his eye warned Jake that if he ordered chicken at the hotel restaurant there would be one less crow on his balcony the next morning. All of the other pilots-maintained poker faces.

Jake took it as a "whiskey talk" lame attempt at humor but dutifully laughed.

In a series of meetings with the creditors including Indian bureaucrats Jake was able to secure lien releases at substantial discounts and thus free up the Sikorsky. Rick Pratt the head pilot who had testified at the Fairbanks trial was on stand-by in Singapore waiting to hear from Jake. When Rick arrived, they celebrated the freeing of the helicopter with some drinks at the Connemara Bar and the following morning Jake returned to Los Angeles.

SINGAPORE & INDONESIA

"Enough is enough—I've had it. Get out of my room and I mean right now".

Jake was screaming at the two Singaporean lawyers who were in his hotel room at the historic Raffles Hotel in Singapore pouring through every document page by page in three very large suitcases that Jake had purchased for the purpose of transporting some records of an Indonesian company to Los Angeles.

Arthur Tang, Camden's Singapore attorney gently took his arm and escorted him to the hallway. "Jake—I don't blame you for losing it, but you have got to calm down. I suggest you go have a martini at the Writers Bar and let me deal with these jerks".

The Writers Bar just off the main lobby at The Raffles was aptly name because luminaries including Noel Coward, Somerset Maugham and Rudyard Kipling had been known to have had their share of cocktails there. This was not to be confused with the Long Bar also at The Raffles where the Singapore Sling was created. By the way it is also legend that a live tiger once wandered into the lobby at The Raffles.

Jake was in the middle of internecine warfare between Camden International Corporation, which owned of 75% of an Indonesian helicopter company and Indonesian individuals who owned the other 25%. The company, Sumatra PT NUH, had been formed and initially capitalized by Camden but under Indonesian law at least 25% of any company doing business there had to be owned by Indonesians. An alliance had been formed with some powerful and influential Indonesians in Jakarta which remained amicable for a couple of years but had fallen apart over—you guessed it—power and money—with each side accusing the other of cooking the books and other management misdeeds. Camden's fleet of 50 helicopters provided logistical support for companies engaged in oil exploration in Indonesia moving men and materials to remote jungle and offshore locations. Most of the operations were in or near the outer islands of Indonesia and thus Camden had offices in Jakarta, but it turned out that Singapore was a better place for its corporate operations.

As he nursed his drink at the Writer's Bar, Jake reflected on what brought him to this dramatic confrontation 9,000 miles from his home in Santa Monica.

⊶╪╀⊷

The dispute between Camden and Sumatra had set the stage for Jake's first trip to Southeast Asia. For years he had heard about the exotic sounding Pan-Am Flight # 1 which traveled around the world. Finally, he was going to take at least the portion of Pan-Am Flight # 1 which goes from Los Angeles to Tokyo to Hong-Kong to Singapore. The first trip one takes to Singapore is somewhat of a shock to the system in that you are traveling for a full twenty-four-hour day and in addition are crossing the international dateline and losing fourteen and a half hours. On Pan-Am Flight # 1 you left Los Angeles at twelve noon and arrived in Singapore a little after midnight t on the second night. Singapore is an island located seventy-five miles north of the equator at the southern tip of Malaysia. Modern Singapore was founded in 1819 by Sir Stamford Raffles and became a part of the British Empire. After breaking with Britain, it became a part of Malaysia and finally in 1965 became the Republic of Singapore, a sovereign nation. Upon his arrival in Singapore Jake checked into the Marco Polo Hotel, a beautiful modern facility located just off Orchard Road which is the main street in Singapore where many hotels, shopping centers and office buildings are located.

Having booked a flight to Jakarta the following afternoon, Jake had the morning to get a quick look at Singapore. He checked with the concierge about the nearest place to go for a run. The concierge suggested the Tanglin District just a few short blocks from the hotel. Jake had found that jogging was an effective way to combine jet lag recovery, fitness and site seeing. He suddenly found himself jogging along a beautiful gently winding tree lined road passing majestic homes and stately Embassies from all over the world including the United States, China, and Israel. He marveled that less than only 36 hours before taking this scenic run he was kissing Laurie goodbye in Santa Monica.

The excitement of being in this beautiful country on a unique business adventure made him forget, well almost forget, about the 90-degree heat combined with 85 degrees of humidity. He had to remind himself how close he was to the Equator.

That afternoon he took a one-and-a-half-hour flight from Singapore to Jakarta. Jakarta is located three hundred miles south of the Equator and is the capital of Indonesia. Indonesia is the fourth largest country in the world with a population of over 260,000,000. It is a huge archipelago containing over 15,000 islands. Jakarta is a large, noisy, and densely populated city.

Although there is a tremendous amount of business and commerce conducted between Singapore and Indonesia and they are only about five hundred miles apart, there are vast cultural differences. Approximately 80% of the people in Singapore are of Chinese extraction and the other 20% consist of Malaysians, Indians, and English. The predominant religions are Buddhism and Christianity. 90% of the people in Indonesia, on the other hand, are Muslims.

Jake checked into the Borobudur Hotel in the heart of Jakarta. The next morning, he took his usual customary run which was anything but usual since it took place on the streets of Jakarta. On almost every street corner there was a woman hunkered down in a squatting position with a display of herbs and spices on the sidewalk hoping for a sale to some passer-by. Jake smiled realizing that if he ever got himself into that squat (which they seemed to be able to maintain for hours) he would never be able to get up. Quite a difference from running on the well-known grassy center divider on San Vicente Boulevard in Santa

Monica and Brentwood taking you past upscale westside homes.

Jake was there for the closing of a loan to Camden to be secured by the helicopters using Aircraft Chattel Mortgages. Before the trip Jake had to learn how to "legalize" a document for use in Indonesia. It was an interesting process which involved having the Mortgages signed before a Notary Public and thereafter having the Los Angeles County Clerk certify that the Notary was in good standing followed by having the California Secretary of State certify the County Clerk. The final step was a visit to the Indonesian Consulate's office on Wilshire Boulevard to get the documents finalized with a fancy gold sticker and blue ribbon. By this time the documents looked very official and could be used in Indonesian transactions.

The closing took place in the law offices of the Indonesian firm representing the lender which was Manufacturers Hanover bank. This was a unique experience in that the law firm occupied a building which had been a residence and the conference room was the dining room. The dining room was beautifully furnished and contained many Indonesian art objects and pictures on the wall, presumably of the ancestors of the senior partners of the firm. The individual Indonesian lawyer representing Manufacturers Hanover looked like a wild man from Borneo. He was dressed very casually in a flowered shirt and white pants. He was a wiry man in his sixties with at least half of his teeth missing and a fierce look in his eyes although he was both friendly and hospitable. Jerry Weinberg the New York lawyer for Manufacturers Hanover was also in attendance. After the closing Jake took Jerry to dinner at a local restaurant which had been recommended called the Oasis. The Oasis again was a converted residence where upon entering the front door two lovely ladies banged a huge gong with large mallets to announce your arrival. Jake offered to pick up the check and was taken back when it came to 55,863 rupiahs. He was relieved to learn that this converts to approximately $80.00 U.S.

After the closing Jake returned to Singapore and then to Los Angeles. At the time of the closing relations between the Americans and Indonesians were still at least superficially friendly and there was no indication whatsoever that the Indonesians did not intend to fulfill the obligations set forth in the documents which they had signed agreeing to make payments in the sum of $50,000 per month to Manufacturers Hanover. The serious problems in Indonesia began within a month after the closing. The first $50,000 payment was not made when due and Jake received a telephone call from Jerry Weinberg requesting the payment. Another payment was missed, and Jake was in constant telephonic communication with the Indonesian office to try and determine the problem in making the payment. He received an incredible variety of excuses from the Indonesians including delays attributed to their religious holiday Ramadan which lasted for 30 days. Finally, the Indonesians attempted to rescind the entire transaction without giving any legal reason whatsoever as to the grounds for rescission. Jake came to learn that the claimed justification for backing out of the Manufacturers Hanover transaction was a long series of grievances against the management of Camden. The grievances including the denial of an inter-company debt from Sumatra PT NUH to Camden, a claim that there was money owing from Camden to the Indonesians, and a claim that Camden was responsible for the failure to meet certain legal and reporting requirements within the country of Indonesia. Much of this was as smoke screen covering up a much more personal feud between Jack McKay the CEO of Camden and Yoko Makarim the CEO of Sumatra over whether McKay was fulfilling duties to his duties to actively participate in the day-to-day management of the company in Indonesia somewhat of a disingenuous claim given the 9,000 miles between Los Angeles and Jakarta.

For five months Camden and Manufacturers Hanover made continuous demands on Sumatra to cure the default and resume the $50,000 monthly payments. Sumatra refused and essentially cut off all communications with the parent company culminating in the purported removal of all Camden personnel from any positions of management or control of the company.

The Indonesians noticed a shareholder meeting of Sumatra in Jakarta for the purpose of officially and legally taking over the management of the company although they were already in physical control. They refused to disclose the date and time for the meeting surprising considering they owned only 25% of the shares.

Jake learned through Indonesian sources that the meeting was going to be somewhere around the middle of May and on May 11, 1981, he traveled to Singapore with a proxy authorizing him to vote the 75% of the Sumatra stock owned by Camden. He contacted Yoko directly by telephone regarding the meeting. Yoko claimed he did not know the specific information and would have to check with his

Attorney. After learning that Jake was in Singapore Yoko set up a meeting at the office of Sumatra's Singapore attorney Henry Guan. Yoko's right-hand man Wijanarko Chonganv (known as Wiji) was there on behalf of the Indonesians. Camden had retained attorney Arthur Tang who was with Baker McKenzie's Singapore office. Arthur attended the meeting representing Camden and Jake. This was the first on many collaborations with Arthur who became a trusted colleague and friend. The ostensible purpose of the meeting was to negotiate a resolution of the outstanding disputes between Camden and Sumatra, but the real reason was to keep Jake in Singapore so that he would not attend a shareholder's meeting scheduled for the next day in Jakarta. Unbeknownst to Wiji, Jake had learned through an attorney in Jakarta who he had been referred to him by Arthur about the date, time, and place of the shareholders meeting (by law it was published in the local newspaper) and had reserved a seat on the last flight from Singapore to Jakarta for that night. He arrived at Henry Guan's office with his bags packed prepared to take a taxi directly from his office to the airport to board the flight to Jakarta.

His seat was in the rear one third of the airplane on the left-hand side and after he took his seat, he saw Wiji board the plane and take a seat approximately six rows in front of him on the far-right hand side of the plane. Since at this point, he did not want Wiji to know that he knew about the meeting and was planning to attend he hid from him during the flight. Jake was able to keep him under surveillance and duck or otherwise get out of view any time that Wiji turned his head in Jake's direction. He even hid his face behind a magazine on a few occasions.

Upon landing in Jakarta, he waited until Wiji left the plane and followed him at approximately two hundred feet so that he would not see him. He successfully avoided him and checked into the Borabudur Hotel in downtown Jakarta. The following morning Jake met Peter Kosumo the Jakarta attorney he had retained through Arthur and briefed him on the situation. Peter agreed to attend the shareholders meeting with him. Unfortunately, Jake did not have a camera to record the look on Wiji's face when he walked in the door with an attorney. He obviously did not expect him and was operating under the assumption that he had been successfully decoyed in Singapore and did not know the actual time and place of the shareholders meeting. It was further obvious that since he was not expected, the Indonesians were not going to even have a physical meeting but rather were going to simply talk to each other over the telephone and adopt such resolutions as were in their interests in connection with legally changing the management and as it turned out the ownership interest of Camden.

Wiji immediately got on the telephone and contacted Yoko, their lawyers and various other individuals who all showed up at Sumatra within about thirty minutes.

Yoko and Jake exchanged pleasantries and superficially Yoko was very polite, however, he was obviously upset about the fact that Camden was persisting to exercise their rights as majority shareholder and would not just go away. Yoko stood about 5"10" appearing to be in his early 40's and looking quite fit and dapper. He wore a gold pin on the lapel of his expensive suit which Jake was to learn to his surprise indicated that he had been voted one of the 10 best dressed men in Indonesia. Who would have thought such a thing?

Jake presented his proxy and although its validity was not challenged the meeting ended up consisting of highly technical arguments between Jake's attorney and the attorneys representing Sumatra regarding procedural matters such as who should chair the meeting, the makeup of the agenda, whether a notary should be present, etc. Although Jake would have liked to have simply taken control of the meeting using the 75% voting power which he had, Peter advised against it and recommended that the meeting be rescheduled with appropriate procedural safeguards to ensure its validity, particularly the presence of a notary public who could record the minutes.

The meeting thus ended without any definite conclusion and Jake had to listen to the list of grievances against Camden. He was at an extreme disadvantage since he had no factual background and was unable to respond to the allegations. All he could do was listen and make notes and report the results of the meeting to Camden's management back in Los Angeles.

At the same time the machinations regarding the shareholders meeting were taking place there was a separate development in Singapore. In the first week of May, Camden had dispatched two former employees who had been retained on a contract basis to Singapore with authorization to take physical control of approximately $1,500,000 worth of helicopter spare parts located at the Singapore facility and ship them back to the United States.

This was being done on the theory that although these helicopter parts were in Singapore for the purpose for providing logistical support to Sumatra, since the Indonesians were denying Camden any management rights and were refusing to honor the inter-company debt it was in the best interest of Camden to ensure its control over the spare parts. At this juncture, the ranks of the employees of the Singapore entity in Singapore were divided in that a few of them were maintaining their loyalty to Camden but others were pledging their allegiance to the Indonesians. Certain of the employees who were in the Indonesian camp found out that the two Camden representatives were taking physical control of the spare parts and immediately notified the Indonesians in Jakarta. The Indonesians' contacted their Singapore lawyer Henry Guan who immediately obtained an order from the Singapore Court enjoining the removal of the spare parts from Singapore.

Jake returned to Los Angeles and within two weeks learned that on May 15th only two days after the abortive shareholders meeting, the Indonesians had purported to remove Jack McKay from his position as President Director of Sumatra. They did this in accordance a procedure set forth in the By-Laws of Sumatra whereby a director can be removed for cause subject to confirmation of such removal at a shareholder meeting within thirty days. Jake therefore knew that they would be scheduling yet another shareholders meeting within thirty days from May 15th to ratify the removal of Jack McKay from office.

Peter Kosumo was monitoring the Jakarta newspapers on behalf of Arthur Tang in order to find out when and where another shareholders meeting was being noticed. Sure enough, on May 30th Peter found a notice in a Jakarta newspaper for a shareholders meeting of Sumatra for June 13th. He let Arthur know Tang who in turn notified Jake of the new meeting date. Because the dispute had escalated to such a high level the senior partners at Peter's Jakarta law firm precipitously withdrew Peter and the firm from any further representation of Camden for reasons that would later become apparent to Jake.

This time, Camden was determined to again attend the meeting with a proxy and this time be fully prepared from a legal standpoint to ensure that the meeting was in fact conducted properly and not only that the efforts to remove Jack McKay from office for cause were stopped but that the legal and physical control on Sumatra could be re-established on behalf of Camden. As of the first week of June, it was planned that Vic Roberts, the CFO and Jake would travel to Jakarta. Vic planned to allow plenty of time to find a new lawyer, hire a notary public and take all other steps to ensure that Camden could regain control at the June 13th meeting.

By this time, due to the cut off of funds from Indonesia, Camden's resources were extremely limited. Approximately three days before the scheduled departures to Jakarta a major creditor of Camden, successfully levied their primary bank account. The "high budget" trip had to be cancelled. The question remained as to whether there could be a "bare bones budget" trip involving fewer people. It was finally decided that Jake would go to Jakarta alone again with a proxy to attend the shareholders meeting. All the activity relating to the levy of the bank account and attempts to remove the levy took up several days and by now it was June 10th only three days before the meeting which was short notice considering the fact that a day is lost in traveling from Los Angeles to Jakarta. Jake departed for Jakarta at midnight on the night of the 10th and traveled straight through for thirty hours to Jakarta via Tokyo, Hong Kong, and Singapore. On a 30-hour flight traveling coach in a crowded airplane one ends up being either sick of or bonded with one's seat mates. Jake was in the middle of a row of three seats. On his left was a guy named Frank who was a sapphire buyer on his way to Sri Lanka to buy precious stones. He told Jake that his experience and expertise enabled him to distinguish 26 different shades of blue with the naked eye. On Frank's last international trip, he was one of the survivors of a crash of two large planes on a runway in Seoul, Korea. Because of this he was popping valium throughout the trip. On Jake's right was a buxom lady named April who was on her way to Jakarta for an engagement as a topless dancer, surprising in a Muslim country. Jake, Frank, and April fortunately bonded, became fast friends even getting beer together at airport layovers.

Jake arrived in Jakarta, exhausted late in the afternoon of the 11th and thus had only one full business day to hire a new lawyer and a notary and otherwise prepare for the shareholders meeting. Early the next morning he went to the American Consulate in Jakarta to discuss the situation both in terms of getting recommendations as to a lawyer and to discuss what by now were considered to be serious risks regarding his personal safety.

Once again, the Indonesians did not know that Camden knew about the time and place of the shareholders meeting. Jake intentionally stayed at the Hotel Indonesia in Jakarta in order that there would be less likelihood that he would be seen. Most American businessmen stay at either the Hilton, the Mandarin, or the Borobudur. It can be difficult for an American company to obtain effective local representation in Jakarta as evidenced by the abrupt withdrawal of Peter Kosumo's firm. Most of the firms will naturally tend to be loyal to their fellow Indonesians and in this case, there was the further problem that Yoko Makarim had a very high profile and was well known in Jakarta. Accordingly, most firms knew him or knew of him and are not anxious to represent interests which are adverse to him.

The American Consulate's office had suggested four attorneys that might be willing to represent Camden under the circumstances described by Jake. After screening three of them over the telephone without any success it was noon the day before the shareholders meeting and Jake was still without a lawyer.

The last lawyer on the list was a Chinese Indonesian named Yap San. Just before noon Jake called Mr. Yap and explained the situation to him. He indicated a willingness to review the case and agreed to meet Jake at two o'clock.

Mr. Yap was Jake's last hope and fortunately he not only agreed to handle the matter but turned out to be a remarkable and extremely competent individual and attorney. The fact that Mr. Yap was a successful lawyer in Jakarta is in and of itself significant. There is tremendous discrimination against the Chinese in Indonesia and in fact people are not supposed to use their Chinese names. Mr. Yap took the position that his name was good enough for his grandfather and father and therefore it was good enough for him and he was not going to change it. He was a small wiry man in his late sixties and Jake immediately felt comfortable with him in that he was tough, competent, and warm. At their two o'clock meeting he immediately grasped the entire situation and understood what needed to be done.

He agreed to line up a notary public and attend the share-holders meeting with Jake.

Jake returned to the Hotel Indonesia after his meeting with Mr. Yap feeling very much relieved that he had finally found a qualified attorney. Jake was sitting in his room at four thirty p.m. when there was a knock on the door. He answered the door and a representative of the Indonesian Police department handed him some papers. The documents were in the Indonesian language and he naturally had no idea what they said, however, the person serving the papers explained that it was a subpoena ordering him to appear at the Indonesian Police station at ten a.m. the following morning the very time set for the shareholders meeting.

This was an incredible development from several standpoints. In the first place Jake did not think the Indonesians knew he was in the country no less where he was staying. Moreover, it was impossible to believe that the order to appear at the Indonesian Police station at the very time set for the shareholders meeting was a mere coincidence. It seemed obvious that the Indonesians had persuaded some low-level police official to prepare a phony subpoena in order to prevent Jake from attending the meeting. He called Mr. Yap to tell him of this development and he told Jake to deliver the subpoena to his office right away.

Mr. Yap reviewed the subpoena and indicated that it was invalid that it did not give any specifics as to why Jake's testimony was required and further did not give three days' notice as required under Indonesian law.

Mr. Yap prepared a letter to the Chief of Police of Indonesia explaining that he represented Jake and that his client had been served with an invalid subpoena. He said that the subpoena would not be honored and that he and Jake would be attending the shareholders meeting.

The following morning Mr. Yap met Jake for breakfast at the hotel and then they went to pick up a notary to attend the meeting at the offices of Sumatra. They arrived at the Sumatra offices a few minutes before 10:00 a.m. It was a Saturday and there was no activity whatsoever on the ground floor where the head office is and where the last meeting had been conducted.

They learned from some security guards that a meeting was taking place on the third floor. When they got off the elevator, they were confronted by guards who indicated that Jake was not to be recognized and would not be allowed to attend the meeting. Yoko, Wiji, their lawyers and others were behind locked doors conducting a meeting. Jake was ordered to sit on a bench in a corridor approximately fifty feet from the door to the room where the meeting was being held. Mr. Yap marched up to the door and knocked loudly demanding entrance. The door opened a crack and Mr. Yap showed the person at the door a copy of a letter authorizing him to represent Jake and a copy of the proxy authorizing Jake to vote 75% of the stock of Sumatra. Mr. Yap was refused admittance and the door was again closed and locked.

Mr. Yap, the notary, and Jake sat on a bench in the corridor discussing their next move. Jake told Mr. Yap that since he had a valid proxy and had traveled nine thousand miles to attend the meeting, he was not going to allow them to get away with keeping him out of the meeting and that if they wouldn't let him into their meeting he would have his own meeting right then and there. He did in fact conduct a meeting (albeit with himself) and proceeded to dismiss the charges against Jack McKay, vote all the Indonesians out of office and elect himself President Director of Sumatra all of this of course with the able guidance of Mr. Yap. He realized that this was perhaps an empty gesture but besides making him feel better it helped create a paper trail that he had in fact showed up at the place and time noticed for the meeting.

At this point, some representatives from the Indonesian Police department got off the elevator and went towards the room where the meeting was being held. Apparently, as a result of Mr. Yap's letter to the Chief of Police, questions had been raised about the invalid subpoena and Yoko and others were being summoned to the Police department to explain themselves.

Yoko, who was later to deny that Jake attended the meeting, walked right by him on his way to the elevator and glared at him. Jake simply said, "Good morning Yoko, how are you?". He replied, "Good morning Jake", said no more and walked right by him.

Mr. Yap, the notary public, and Jake then took a taxi to the notary's office to document the meeting which Jake had conducted by himself by preparing minutes of the meeting and duly certifying them in accordance with Indonesian law.

By this time Jake was very nervous and somewhat paranoid about the Indonesians and accordingly had Mr. Yap personally escort him to the airport and stood by until he was aboard the plane headed back for Singapore.

Another purpose of the trip, besides attending the shareholders meeting, was to obtain certain important records of both the Singaporean and the Indonesian entities which were stored at the Singapore facility and bring them back with him to Los Angeles. When Jake got back to Singapore, he checked in to the Raffles Hotel and the next morning went out with Arthur Tang to Salida which is the Singapore Air Force air base where Sumatra's Singapore office was located.

Arthur and Jake loaded the trunk of Arthur's car with some of the records and took them all to Arthur's home to sort through the file to determine which files should in fact be brought back to the United States.

The next morning Jake went back to Salida to obtain more records and while he was loading them into the trunk of a rented car a Singapore Police car pulled up and two uniformed officers served him with a court order purporting to enjoin him from moving any records from Singapore. By this time Jake was very tired of being harassed in both Indonesia and Singapore and he argued vociferously with the police that the order was not valid and did not cover the records which he was taking.

This was an extremely unusual assignment for these particular Police officers, and they were at a loss as to what to do because they were being embroiled in a civil dispute. All they knew was that they had this court order and their boss had told them not to let Jake take the records so they did not want him to leave for fear that they would get into trouble.

They called their supervisor and Jake called Arthur Tang and both Arthur and their supervisor were on their way to Salida at the same time. Salida is a forty-minute drive from downtown Singapore and approximately an hour went by before anything happened. Jake was tired of all the non-sense and decided to simply leave.

The Police officers became extremely upset and still didn't want him to leave. Jake got in the car and was starting the engine when their supervisor pulled up. Shortly thereafter Arthur Tang arrived as did Henry Guan the Indonesian's Singapore lawyer. Henry started to pore over the documents and after two hours of discussions Arthur persuaded the police that the records were not covered by the court order and therefore Jake should be allowed to leave.

Arthur and Jake took the records back to Jake's hotel room at the Raffles. The records were packed in three large suitcases which weighed one hundred pounds each. By this time Arthur had been contacted again by Henry Guan resulting in a long negotiation about the court order and the scope of the injunction and Jake's right to remove the records from Singapore. Arthur, by way of compromise, offered to let Henry and an associate attorney inspect the records in Jake's hotel room so that they would at least know what he was taking and would be able to eventually argue in court as to whether or not the records were covered by the court order.

Relying on Arthur's advice Jake reluctantly agreed, and a meeting was arranged for his hotel room at 6:00 p.m. that night. Jake was extremely annoyed by the whole thing particularly since Henry had been at Salida when the Singapore Police were there and had already seen many of the records. He started going through the same records again page by page basis which would have taken forever. This all led up to the moment when Jake lost it and Arthur gently suggested that he head for the Writer's bar.

At 8:30 p.m. Jake called the room Arthur told him that Guan and his associate were still carefully going through the records and had only scratched the surface. Jake ran out of patience and stormed back into the room and ordered Guan and his associate to leave in a very forceful manner. This time the normally very calm Arthur who was also out of patience did not try to restrain Jake. They did in fact leave and to Jake's relief he was not confronted by any more Singapore Police or other legal action prior to getting on the plane to Los Angeles the following morning with all the records.

After his return to Los Angeles Jake was to learn that the Indonesians had prepared a set of minutes covering their version of what they claimed happened at the June 13th shareholders meeting. Their version of the minutes stated that he did not show up and that the charges against Mr. McKay were confirmed and that therefore he was out of office. They went to state that the sole directors were now Yoko and Wiji.

Thus, there were two conflicting sets of minutes and in order to resolve the legal control of Sumatra it would be necessary to either notice another shareholders meeting at Jakarta and undo the damage that the Indonesians have done or seek remedies through the Indonesian courts.

Jake was feeling quite self-satisfied as he sipped a martini on the Singapore Airlines flight to Los Angeles. After all he had defied legal maneuvering and Police Departments in two countries and was returning with three huge suitcases of books and records which would presumably be of great value in connection with any further proceedings. Imagine his shock when after disembarking from the exhausting

30-hour flight he was greeted by a process server and handed a Deposition Subpoena for the Production of Documents ordering him to produce all of the books and records of Sumatra within 15 days at the offices of Montgomery & Kraft then the largest law firm in Los Angeles.

It turned out that while Jake was chasing around Singapore and Indonesia the implosion of Camden had continued unabated. The management of Camden had kept Jake uninformed in what charitably could be attributed to "leaving him alone" so he could do what he could abroad but in actuality was a combination of panic, denial and just plain giving up on salvaging anything out of Camden's meager remaining business and assets. A proxy fight had been initiated by two individuals named Rob McDonald and Bob Jacobs who were affectionately known in corporate and financial circles as just Rob & Bob. Rob & Bob had mastered the art of hostile take overs while Jake didn't even know what a proxy fight was. It turns out that any shareholders with at least five percent of the stock in a publicly held corporation could launch an effort to solicit proxies from other shareholders and if successful gain majority control, oust the current management and take over the company. Rob & Bob had enough money and were smart enough to retain Montgomery & Kraft a firm with a high level of expertise in such matters. With the help of some sleuthing their attorney had somehow found out about the records being brought back and obviously even Jake's flight information.

The management and Board of Directors were leaving Camden like the proverbial rats deserting a sinking ship. In an odd gesture Jake had been appointed to the Board and was basically the last man standing. Jake obviously did not have the resources to oppose the proxy fight but in a bold move contacted Rob & Bob and suggested that they meet. He convinced them that if anything could be salvaged out of Camden they would need his background and knowledge and proposed that they drop the proxy fight and in return he would appoint them to the Board provided that they would keep him on the Board and see what they could salvage together. He of course had run this scenario by Vic Roberts and Vic who had been among those bailing from the company told him to "go for it".

Over the next several weeks Jake came to know Rob & Bob very well. Considering that they had started out as bitter rivals it was remarkable how quickly they became friends. Jake immediately could see why Rob & Bob were so successful. They were a perfect example of a classic marriage of complimentary skill sets. Bob was the cerebral partner a quiet thinker and strategist while Rob was the extroverted salesman who could charm his way into a deal. They invited Jake into their elegant homes in the most prestigious part of Pasadena where Jake and Laurie were wined and dined by Rob & Bob and their families.

Rob & Bob did not become wealthy by pursuing lost causes and they quickly decided that the three of them would travel to Singapore and Indonesia to see if anything could be salvaged for Camden. After several grueling trips to Southeast Asia flying coach on Camden's bare bones budget what a contrast it was to travel first class with Rob & Bob. Without apology Rob & Bob lived high on the hog with Bob even bringing an expensive bottle of champagne for the three of them to share. This was the 1980's when airline travel was actually fun. No TSA, no shoe removal before boarding and a genuine party atmosphere particularly on long international flights.

There was a very awkward element to the three of them traveling together to meet with Yoko, Wiji and the other Sumatra personnel who had gone to war with Camden. Bringing Jake was risky since he had become persona non grata as far as Sumatra was concerned and was perceived as the "evil" attorney for "evil" clients. Rob & Bob had thought this through, and Jake understood that he would remain in the hotel for much of the trip while Rob & Bob played their white knight rescuer card with Yoko and Wiji.

In a series of meetings in both Singapore and Indonesia Rob & Bob despite their considerable skills basically could not budge Yoko and Wiji from their position that they claimed was supported by Indonesian law to the effect that Camden had been legally ousted and had no further interest in Sumatra. In a bizarre gesture of "good will" Yoko offered to have Rob & Bob spend a weekend in Bali as his guests at a hotel where he held a majority ownership interest. Rob & Bob did a cost-benefit analysis and after conferring with attorneys in both Los Angeles and Indonesia determined that the value of the by now limited remaining assets did not justify the costs and efforts of litigating in Indonesia. To salvage something out of a 18,000-mile round trip they took Yoko up on his offer and spent a memorable weekend in Bali before heading home. As a slap in the face to Jake, Yoko provided a Presidential Suite to Rob & Bob and the smallest room in the hotel for Jake. Rob & Bob graciously invited Jake to spend as much time as he wanted in their palatial digs.

On their last day Rob & Bob rented motor scooters to tour around Bali and Jake opted to pass and just hang around Kuta Beach a world-renowned surfing Mecca close to the hotel. He learned that if you order a mushroom omelet in Kuta Beach you may end up hallucinating and thus Jake spent a pleasant afternoon sitting on the beach seeing geometric patterns along with the crashing surf. Jake had smoked his share of marijuana some years before and had even tried hashish a few times but schrooms, as they are called, had a much bigger impact but at least a very pleasant impact.

Thus ended Jake's adventures in Southeast Asia on a rather anti-climactic note but nonetheless with some experiences he would never forget.

ANDRE DEVRIES

Thrust back into private practice by the demise of Camden it didn't take long for Jake to reconnect with some old clients and acquire some new cases. He saw an ad in the Los Angeles Daily Journal about an office for lease within a suite in Marina Del Rey. After meeting with Bruce Augustine, the lawyer who held the lease Jake happily took the space which was on the eighth floor of a building that was less than five miles from Jake's home and featured a gorgeous view of the Marina and the ocean. Jake was one of eight lawyers in the suite each with a different specialty thus facilitating the referral of cases to one another which was an ideal arrangement combining some cost sharing and other benefits of a firm even though it was a collection of eight solo practitioners. Within a year Bruce took off to become a "ski bum" in Sun Valley, Idaho, and Jake took over the master lease.

On a Tuesday morning he received a telephone call from his sister Deborah who told him she and her husband needed to meet with him as soon as possible. Jake was close to Deborah and sensing the urgency in her voice asked if he should stop by their home after work. He could hear the sigh of relief in Deborah's voice so grateful that he was coming over that night.

Deborah was two years older than Jake but you would never know it when they were growing up together. Up until the third grade they were about the same size and some people thought they were twins because of their habit of finishing each other's sentences. A solemn ritual occurred when they were asked to share a bottle of Coke. One would pour the contents into two glasses right next to each other and the other would carefully monitor to make sure each person's share was at precisely the same height.

Deborah's husband Dirk DeVries and Jake had developed a close friendship more like blood brothers than in-laws. On arrival after giving Jake a warm hug Deborah poured a glass of wine and the three of them sat down in the living room. Dirk got right to the point. His father Andre DeVries had died very suddenly of a massive heart attack. There had been no prior warning—it was one of those afflictions where the first symptom was sudden death.

Dirk and Andre had been estranged for many years following Andre's divorce from Dirk's mother Gertrude when Dirk was eight. Dirk was born in The Netherlands and came to the United States with his mother after her divorce from Andre. Andre was a brilliant scientist who ended up working as a Food Chemist a highly specialized niche involving among other things formulating pet food products. At the time of his death he was living and working in Puerto Rico. During the two years prior to Andre's death there had been somewhat of a rapprochement with Dirk to the point where Dirk and Deborah visited him in Puerto Rico. Dirk's loyalty would of course always be with his mother Gertrude who had raised him alone with some financial but no emotional support from Andre.

Dirk as the only child would be the sole inheritor of any assets left behind by Andre. The only problem was that Andre not only left no will, but he also left no detailed records of what he owned or where any assets were located. In their visit to Puerto Rico and through other communications with Andre, Dirk had learned that Andre had accumulated a considerable amount of wealth and had assets scattered throughout several countries.

Jake immediately knew his visit was not only to commiserate with Dirk and Deborah about Andre's death but in his role as the family lawyer. Dirk had followed Jake's career ever since his marriage to Deborah and was aware of his legal skills and perhaps more important his obvious love of the detective work associated with any case he handled.

In very short order Dirk and Jake reached an agreement that Jake would undertake a search for Andre's assets, that they would share all out-of-pocket expenses fifty/fifty and that Jake's fee would be 25% of whatever was found.

After the meeting Dirk and Deborah traveled to Puerto Rico to attend Andre's funeral and while there gained access to his apartment and were able to search through his records which although very sparse did include a few clues. On their return Dirk and Jake met to go over the files Dirk had brought back.

Prior to being assigned to a position in Puerto Rico, Andre had worked at the company headquarters in San Diego. In going through the files Jake saw correspondence between Andre and a Tom Johnston who was a colleague at work who had become a friend of Andre's. Jake thought it would be worth it to make a visit to Mr. Johnston in San Diego. A meeting was set up and Jake introduced himself to Tom as the attorney for Andre's son. Tom was friendly enough, but the meeting went nowhere in that Tom didn't seem to have any information about any assets that might have been owned by Andre. Like a scene in so many detective television shows Jake ended the meeting by handing Tom his card: "Here's my card. If you happen to come across anything that might be of interest, please give me a call".

Wouldn't you know it—about two weeks later on a Monday Jake got a call from Tom.

"I was cleaning out my garage over the weekend and I found a letter that could be of interest". "Would you mind reading it to me?" replied Jake with anticipation.

It turned out that the letter was a copy of correspondence to Andre from a Poul Nielsen, a banker in Copenhagen, Denmark, that somehow found its way into a file of Tom's. The letter stated, among other things, that Poul was looking forward to hearing from Andre regarding "the matters we have been discussing". Jake tried to hide his excitement as he asked Tom to fax him a copy of the letter.

Early the next morning when it was mid-afternoon in Denmark, Jake called Poul Nielsen and introduced himself. Poul who had learned of Andre's untimely death said: "I was hoping someone would call me". This is getting increasingly like a "B" movie thought Jake. Poul only said enough to indicate that he had information that was extremely confidential and thought an in-person meeting would be appropriate. That was enough for Jake—after telling Dirk about this development he was on a plane to Copenhagen within forty-eight hours. Before leaving he prepared a detailed Power of Attorney and Authorization Letter which he had Dirk sign before a Notary Public authorizing Jake to act on behalf of Dirk as to all matters possibly relating to the Estate of Andre DeVries.

Jake checked into the Hotel du Nord which Poul had suggested as being less than a kilometer from United Bank of Denmark (UBD) Bank where Poul was a senior international banker. It was located on The Stroget which is known as one of the longest pedestrian streets (no vehicles allowed) in the world extending for about 3.2 kilometers.

The following morning Jake arrived at UBD and was greeted by a receptionist who escorted him to Poul's elegantly furnished office. Sometimes when people from totally diverse cultures meet for the first time there is a magical instant rapport which cannot be defined but can only be felt. Such was the case with Poul and Jake. Their initial handshake was the beginning of what would be a wonderful professional and personal friendship which would last for years to come. Poul was seventy-eight years old, but you could never tell and as Jake would discover his physical fitness would put most younger people to shame.

Poul was full of life and Jake would soon learn that he spoke seven languages most of them including French and English very fluently. When he had gotten to know Poul Jake asked him: "Poul, when you answer the telephone how do you know what language to speak?" "Easy" said Poul—"I just say Allo and once I see what language they are speaking I simply join them".

Poul was very shrewd but in a good way and spent the entire morning sizing up Jake to test his level of trust and then invited him to lunch after which he indicated they could discuss Andre's business affairs. Following a two-hour lunch and a shared bottle of wine at a fancy restaurant frequented by upscale Danish businesspeople Poul and Jake made their way back to UBD where Jake found out about the real Andre DeVries story.

Through a banking connection in Amsterdam he had learned about Poul and his reputation for discretely helping people hide their assets in a secure and yet totally legal manner. It seems that Andre was extremely secretive about his affairs and had engaged Poul to serve as Trustee with control over approximately $1,000,000 US with instructions to deposit $500,000 into safe, secure (and secret) bank accounts and the other $500,000 into European real estate.

In order to make sure the entire $500,000 was both insured and less likely to attract scrutiny either from Danish authorities or the IRS Poul had opened 30 separate trust accounts in his name as Trustee with Andre as the beneficiary. At Andre's direction he had named Dirk as the secondary beneficiary. Under Danish law up to 100,000 kroner (at the time about $15,000 U.S.) could be held in a Danish bank account with no requirement to report the account to the Danish government or to anyone else. Poul was a very dedicated devotee of Wagnerian Opera. Each year he would travel to Bayreuth, Germany, to attend the Wagnerian Opera Festival. He suggested to Andre and Andre agreed to put each of the accounts in the name of a character from one of Wagner's operas. Jake already knew he liked Poul, and this was more than confirmed when he saw dozens of bank pass books with names like Tristan DeVries, Isolde DeVries, Siegfried DeVries and on and on.

As to the real estate Poul suggested and Andre agreed that a good investment would be in Nice, France which happened to be near a Villa that Poul owned in Antibes and thus was an area where he personally had knowledge about real estate values.

Andre had recently contacted Poul to have him designate Dirk as the sole beneficiary. It was a combination of Dirk being the only rightful heir, the recent reuniting of father and son and assuaging his guilt for the many years of neglect following the divorce from Gertrude. Poul was just beginning his search to track down Dirk when he received the telephone call from Jake. Because Andre's death was very sudden and unexpected—he was 58 years old—there had not yet been an opportunity for Poul to obtain any information about Dirk or his whereabouts thus his relief hearing from Jake.

Poul indicated that the logistics for transferring the money and the property in Nice could be discussed the next day and in the meantime despite the already two-hour lunch suggested that Jake go relax at the hotel for a while and meet him for dinner at 7:00 p.m.

On his return to his room at the Hotel du Nord Jake collapsed on the bed and let what he had just learned sink in. He thought of many of his law school classmates who were handling auto accident cases or divorces or sitting in high rise office buildings being pressured to bill at least 160 hours a month to insurance companies and other big corporate clients. When he compared that to his adventures in India, Singapore, Indonesia and now Denmark he felt pretty good about it. He was on the verge of collecting $500,000 for Dirk and his share would be $125,000 not to mention what might be worked out about the property in Nice—not bad for a quick trip to Copenhagen.

Poul had asked him to meet in front of Det Lille Apotek one of the oldest and most historically significant restaurants in Copenhagen. Poul really knew how to live. After descending a narrow dark staircase, they arrived in a dining room the likes of which Jake had never seen. They proceeded to have a five-course meal with a different wine served with each course. Feeling no pain Poul tantalized Jake by telling him he had something else important to tell him, but it could wait until the next morning. After dinner Poul had Jake stop by his apartment in a beautiful 100-year-old building whereupon Poul sat down at a piano and played a minuet.

On Jake's arrival at UBD the following morning Poul explained that as to the 30 bank accounts it would take some time to arrange for a transfer of the money. Jake gave him information needed for a wire transfer of the money to Jake's clients' trust account the following week. Jake had discovered that when doing business in a foreign country it was important to adapt to local customs and mores as much as possible and not to behave like a heavy-handed over-kill American lawyer. He and Poul jointly drafted a simple memorandum documenting what they had discussed.

Poul mentioned that he had a summer Villa in Antibes, France, and invited Jake to visit him there with his wife and go together to nearby Nice to see the property he had purchased in trust for Andre and meet both the attorney and the real esate broker he had retained to assist in purchasing and managing the property. It turned out that Poul was planning to retire from banking soon and live permanently in Antibes. Of the seven languages he spoke French was clearly his favorite to both speak and read and he loved the people of Southern France.

In his junior year at Occidental College, a small liberal arts school in Los Angeles, Jake was walking from the library at one end of a very Ivy League looking quad to the Student Union at the other end of the quad. Walking toward him was a very attractive young girl wearing an outfit comprised of a garment that could only be described as a cross between Bermuda shorts and overalls with a white blouse beneath the straps of the green shorts. One strap had dropped from her shoulder to her waist. Although a total stranger Jake approached her and gently lifted the strap back to her shoulder where it belonged. The gesture was in no means intended as an inappropriate or too personal touching and the young woman seeming to appreciate the kind gesture smiled and said "thank you". Jake shyly introduced himself and asked her name. "Laurie" she replied equally as shyly. That moment of mutual trust and understanding which lasted for less than 30 seconds was a prophetic metaphor for a relationship that would lead to romance, marriage and a life-long relationship. Laurie stood about 5'2" with lovely light brown hair and gorgeous blue-green eyes. Jake boldly asked if she would like to have a cup of coffee and Laurie accepted his invitation.

Jake and Laurie became inseparable. Both good students they hung out together in the library stacks each studying their own material and taking breaks together. After dating for three years they married between Jake's first and second year of law school. Laurie enrolled in graduate school while Jake finished up law school, earned her PhD in clinical psychology and became an excellent psychotherapist. Laurie's incredible intuition (sometimes scary – like reading your mind) and in depth knowledge of just about every form of psychopathology was a blessing and he could always count on her as a sounding board and to help size up people he encountered throughout his career.

On his return to Santa Monica Jake brought Dirk, Deborah & Laurie up to date on the results of his trip to Copenhagen and discussed the need to travel to Nice (big sacrifice) to see the property and work out the details regarding the transfer to Dirk. He naturally suggested that Dirk and Deborah join them, but they had to defer due to other family and business commitments.

Two weeks later on arrival in Antibes Jake was greeted warmly like an old friend and Laurie and Poul took to each other immediately. Poul's Villa was in the hills of Antibes with a view of the Mediterranean. They spent two leisurely days with side trips to the Provence where so many French impressionists had spent time perfecting their craft. Their room at Poul's Villa featured a balcony looking out at the water and down to Nice where in the evening you could see a beautifully lighted up Ferris Wheel at a park near the sea.

Jake and Laurie quickly found out the secret to Poul's youthful appearance and vigor. He started each morning with a series of vigorous calisthenics followed by a breakfast that defied conventional medicine. It was comprised of a soft-boiled egg, a piece of very strong cheese and a shot of bitters (yes—alcohol) and of course a cup of strong coffee. Jake and Laurie gamely joined in on the bitters—after all they had to be gracious guests. This was followed by a four-mile round trip walk to Carrefour, part of a French owned supermarket chain. The villa was near the top of the hills and Carrefour near the bottom and thus the walk back up hill with a bag of groceries was quite challenging. Essentially Poul had tremendous Joie de Vivre and that is what kept him young.

It was time to meet Michel Dubois an attorney and Claude Bernard a real estate broker in Nice both of whom had been retained by Poul to assist in finding a suitable real esate investment to purchase as the Trustee for Andre. Driving on a narrow steep winding road down from Poul's villa Poul expertly honked his horn strategically at every turn as was the custom to warn oncoming drivers and they made it safely to the Towne Centre of Antibes and then on to Nice.

They met Michel and Claude at the bar at Hotel Negresco on the Promenade des Anglais. The Negresco is a historic pink colored architecturally beautiful building constructed in 1912 which was a favorite of the rich and famous. Even the Beatles had stayed there in their heyday. Michel and Claude were charming, and Jake and Laurie soon discovered that the French don't get down to business until after sharing a bottle of wine. Sipping a glass of wine and looking across the Promenade des Anglais to the beautiful beach and sea not to mention a lot of gorgeous women it occurred to Jake that in his next life he wouldn't mind being French. Claude explained residential real estate in Nice and the tremendous investment it is due to the strong rental market not only in peak summer months but throughout the year. Michel and Claude were a good team in that Michel could handle the transfer of title to Dirk and Claude was happy to stay on as the property manager handling rentals. Jake and Laurie were nearly jumping out of their skin anxiously awaiting a viewing of the house that Poul and Claude between them had selected and purchased on behalf of Andre and which would end up being owned by Dirk to be held for investment or even lived in as a second home. They learned that you just don't rush French people especially at the Cote D'Azur which might help explain why a Mediterranean lifestyle is considered to be healthy compared to the America hyperkinetic constant rushing.

Finally, after polishing off a second bottle of wine Michel and Claude were ready to escort Jake and Laurie to the property. It was well worth the wait—a stunning villa nestled in the hills within five minutes of the heart of Nice. A beautiful winding stone stairway led from the street up a gradual slope to the two-story home which was a little masterpiece with solid stone construction that had stood the test of time since it was built over 100 years ago. The home was currently occupied by a short-term tenant who when notified by Claude had graciously made the home available for inspection. The crowning feature was a lovely front terrace with a view of the sea. While touring the home Jake and Laurie glanced at each other and smiled with a look that said, "We could live here." Jake shouldn't have been surprised at the wonderful choice Poul had made as an investment for Andre which would now be passed on to Dirk. After enthusiastically thanking Michel and Claude and exchanging European style hugs complete with air kisses to each cheek, Poul, Jake and Laurie headed back to Antibes.

Chez Jay's was a popular local watering hole strategically located diagonally across from the Santa Monica pier. Jake had discovered Jay's as a good place to wind down after a long day in trial at the Santa Monica courthouse a few short blocks away. Jay's was not at all fancy but was truly unique. The owner Jay Fiondello was the consummate host and greeter. Two very different types frequented the place. There were the regulars sitting at the bar comprised of local Santa Monica characters many of them alcoholics who treated Jay's as their home away from home. The dining section on the other hand was frequented by more upscale clientele including the rich and famous. Among the regulars were Johnny Carson, Lee Marvin and occasionally Frank Sinatra. There were a series of small booths across from the bar and one more private booth towards the rear which Jay called the Kissinger Room since it was where he would seat Henry Kissinger and his guests who would show up from time to time.

Jay's was one of the first places to always have baskets of peanuts in the shell on the bar and at the tables. Guests were encouraged to discard the shells on the floor where they would accumulate in some saw dust to be swept away each night. Jay always the marketeer once talked astronaut Alan Shepard into taking a peanut to the moon and bringing it back where it resided in Jay's Safe Deposit box. Jay's was also the place where Daniel Ellsberg, who at the time was working for The Rand Corporation next door, is said to have passed the Pentagon Papers to a newspaper reporter. Marlon Brando on one occasion arrived at Jay's alone and waltzed off with one of the waitresses.

Jake was well known at Jay's and had become the unofficial attorney who would deal with legal problems that would arise. The day-to-day operations of Jay's were conducted by Jay's mother Alice who was a permanent resident at a motel across the parking lot. She once called Jake frantically and asked him to come right over to deal with the arrest of one of the bus boys for possession of marijuana. Jay's had an old fashion jukebox where for a quarter you could select a song and press the right buttons. Other regulars could tell when Jake was there since he invariably inserted his quarter and pressed 4Q which was Bunny Berigan playing his trumpet and with his raspy voice singing *"I can't get started with you."*

On Jake and Laurie's return from Southern France Jay's seemed to be a fitting place to have dinner with Dirk and Deborah to celebrate the discovery of both the bank accounts in Copenhagen and the villa in Nice. He called Jay and asked him to reserve the Kissinger Room for the occasion. He had kept Dirk apprised on the situation with daily phone calls, but it was time to get down to the details concerning both the money and the property.

Jake of course knew all the waitresses and when Julie greeted the group at their table she smiled at Jake and said: "Bombay Sapphire up with two olives?" He nodded in agreement and asked her to bring a wine list to his brother-in-law Dirk gesturing across the table.

Jake started the conversation by offering to reduce his fee. "I didn't have to do much and didn't have to sue anyone. 25% seems like a lot for two wonderful trips to Europe. Poul is a very responsible person, and I am sure he would have tracked you down eventually without my help." Dirk would have none of it. "You earned every penny. You discovered the letter from Poul, took the initiative to go immediately to Copenhagen and otherwise made all of this happen. Besides, we are all family—when the money arrives in your trust account you can disburse my 75% to me and retain your 25% fee. As to the villa, you and Laurie will have unlimited use of it as a get-away during any trips to Europe."

Thus, the matter was settled, and arrangements were made for Dirk and Deborah to visit Poul in Antibes and sit down with Michel and Claude to finalize the title transfer. Based on Jake and Laurie's recommendation they had already decided to keep Claude on as the property manager. They could of course always contact him and reserve time for their own enjoyment of the villa or for use by Jake and Laurie. Guilt can be a wondrous thing . After years of neglect, Andre had managed to make a positive change in the life of Dirk and his family.

LANZAROTE

About six months after the conclusion of Jake's work on the Andre DeVries matter, he got an unexpected call from Poul Nielsen. At their first meeting in Copenhagen Poul had mentioned that he had lived in the United States for a year back in the 1930's while participating in a graduate program at Columbia University in Manhattan and hadn't been to New York since. He was planning a return visit after all those years and wondered if Jake could meet him there. Poul off handedly mentioned a business matter he would like to discuss with Jake that had nothing to do with Andres DeVries. Intrigued and always looking for an excuse to go to New York, Jake and Poul arranged the details as to when and where to meet.

Jake was born in New Rochelle which as the song says is 45 minutes from Broadway in Westchester County. Laurie would good naturedly kid him: "For God's Jake why do you think of yourself as a New Yorker – your parents moved the family to California when you were seven years old.?" Jake had two answers. Early childhood memories are very powerful. Who could forget being taken to the Automat by your grandparents, putting a quarter in a slot and seeing a piece of pie magically appear behind a little door? Then there was the Macy's Thanksgiving Day Parade, the Christmas tree and ice rink at Rockefeller Center, the top of the Empire State Building, and Yankee Stadium where his older brother took him to see his first baseball game when he was four years old. Years later in his stint at Camden International, before the Southeast Asia adventures, he got another heavy dose of Manhattan in a series of trips for meetings with bankers. He had developed his Manhattan routine which included a stay at The Plaza, dinner at one of his favorite hangouts which included Café des Artistes, Sardi's and of course Elaine's on the Upper East Side. Still a runner, one of Jakes favorites jogs covered five miles from the front door of the Plaza up though Central Park for a lap around the reservoir and back to the Plaza. The trip and meeting were quickly arranged. Poul readily accepted Jake's suggestion to stay at The Plaza. Laurie, although she did not share Jake's passion for New York, was excited about seeing Poul again and about revisiting the wonderful unparalleled museums the city had to offer. After exchanging warm embraces, the three of them headed for Café des Artistes for dinner and a chance to get down to business.

Poul explained that he was concerned about a substantial investment he had made in the Canary Islands and wanted to retain Jake to investigate the matter. The reason he selected Jake was due to knowing that he had a flair for detective work and also, he didn't want to incur the embarrassment of disclosing to any Danish professional colleagues that he may have made a foolish investment since he was in the business of giving investment advice to others. Jake was a safe and friendly choice as someone he could trust. His investment was in a proposed housing development on the Island of Lanzarote. When Jake confessed to Poul that he didn't know anything about the Canary Islands – not even where they were, it was agreed that dinner would be devoted to Canary Islands/Lanzarote 101 and an overview of Poul's investment with the details to be left to meetings the next day. Poul explained that the Canaries are an archipelago and part of Spain but much closer to Africa than to Europe. In fact, they were about 1400 miles from Spain and only about 75 miles from North Africa. Lanzarote is the fourth largest of the islands and had become an extremely popular resort for Western Europeans particular Danes seeking relief from the chilly winter months. Enter Lars Jensen who had raised money from Poul and others for a housing development on Lanzarote. The idea sounded good – an attractive village near the beach with lovely cottages to serve as either retirement or second homes for sun-starved Danes. The project had stalled, and Lars had gone silent on him failing to respond to multiple inquiries. The three of them agreed to stop after the brief overview to enjoy the rest of the evening and have Poul and Jake resume in the next day while Laurie was out visiting the Metropolitan Museum of Art and the Guggenheim.

The following morning Jake met with Pouf at his room and got the whole story. Poul showed him what was the Spanish version of what Jake knew as a Private Placement Memorandum (PPM). PPM's are typically 30-40 pages long with about a five-page Executive Summary. Usually, the longest section of a PPM is entitled Risk Factors where prospective investors are warned about multiple risks and informed that they could well lose their money. It covers potential costs overruns, negative market conditions and a host of other factors which amount to CYA for the syndicator putting the deal together. By contrast the Executive Summary is the hard-core sales pitch painting a rosy picture with projections showing potential huge returns on the investment. There is nothing wrong per se with PPM's but as a practical matter most investors focus on the Executive Summary which includes a lot of pretty pictures and gloss over the rest including the all-important risk factors.

Jensen had raised $250,000 each from Poul and seven others for a total of $2,000,000. For the first year there were glowing monthly reports about finalizing the design, getting the project approved, and obtaining bids from subcontractors. When the reports stopped coming Poul remembered that during his last visit with Poul in Antibes Jake had regaled Poul with stories about two projects in Santa Monica in which he was not only the attorney but one of the developers working with a close friend who was an architect. An attorney who was also a developer and a self-styled detective seemed like an ideal candidate to deal with Lars Jensen.

Jake knew it was especially important to discuss with Poul his recommended strategy before moving forward with a retainer agreement. In some cases, the widespread practice of starting off with a formal attorney demand letter does not make sense, and this was clearly one of them. Such demands are normally met with a response from an attorney denying any wrongdoing followed by stonewalling and protracted delays followed by expensive litigation. Jake's strategy was to confront people directly, catch them off guard and get as much information as possible before going into a formal adversarial mode. Of course, all of this is easier said than done but Poul readily agreed with the approach and a formal retainer agreement was quickly negotiated with Poul covering all out-of-pocket expenses and the fee to be a percentage of the amount recovered. It was understood of course that if Jake were unsuccessful in getting a satisfactory resolution with Lars, Poul would have to hire a Spanish attorney in the Canary Islands.

Once comfortably seated on their American Airlines flight to Madrid via Dallas, Jake turned to Laurie, took her hand, and smiled: "We are off to quite an adventure". "I guess that's what I signed up for", Laurie replied. From Madrid they would fly via Iberia Express to Arrecife Airport now called Cesar Manrique Airport after an artist and architect who was a revered figure on Lanzarote as they were soon to learn.

On the flight to Madrid Jake reviewed what he had learned from Poul and from carefully studying the investment documents. The company Poul had invested in was Haria Village Homes, SL which was set up as a *Sociedad Limitada*, the Spanish equivalent of a limited liability company. Lars Jensen was the Managing Member while Poul and the other investors were silent partners. Jake had learned that Haria Village Homes had a sales office at the site where the homes were to be built.

As much as they might have enjoyed an overnight in Madrid, Jake and Laurie had chosen to power straight through to Lanzarote. This turned out to be no hardship at all since they were able to spend an hour layover at the Madras Barajas Terminal 4 designed by Architect Antonio Lamela featuring a futuristic colorful canopy enveloping the entire terminal. They enjoyed a snack of Tapas (what else?) and some lovely Spanish wine before boarding the two-and-a-half-hour flight on Iberia Express to Lanzarote. Their seatmate in a row of three turned out to be a charming gentleman named Romeo Zapata who was returning to his home in Lanzarote. Laurie took the window seat; Jake was in the center and Romeo was on the aisle. Romeo appeared to be in his late 30's possibly early 40's obviously very fit with a light beard, a full head of hair, and piercing eyes looking like he could be a leading man. Far from conceited he was down to earth and talkative. As luck would have it, he was born and raised in Haria and very proud of his hometown.

Jake had done as much research as he could – this was before the Internet and Google – and thus Romeo was the perfect source for some valuable information during the flight. He shared with Jake and Laurie the colorful history stressing the contribution of Cesar Manrique. Haria was known as the Valley of a Thousand Palms from an age-old custom of planting a palm tree every time a baby was born. In what would now be clearly politically incorrect the custom was to plant two trees if a boy and one tree if a girl. Romeo asked what brought them to Haria and Jake, not wanting to spill too many beans, replied that they were going to look at a project called Haria Valley Homes and wondered if Romeo knew anything about it. Romeo, very relaxed until that moment, visibly flinched. He told Jake it started out as a well-planned very promising project but was currently on hold and had been for at least six months. He elaborated that the developer had defaulted in payments to subcontractors and suppliers and was rumored to be out of money. The result was a jobsite with partially completed homes in the initial stages of framing. It was obviously an uncomfortable topic for Romeo. Jake marveled at the odds that towards the end of a 20-hour journey he would be seated next to someone with knowledge about the project he had set out to investigate. With a nod to Laurie, he decided to trust his instincts and disclose the reason for his visit. His candor encouraged reciprocal candor from Romeo who told Jake he had been a project superintendent and had been laid off. So, there it was – another "common enemy" scenario.

Romeo informed them that there was indeed a small sales office which was a beautiful miniature version of the homes that were to be built. There was a very competent sales lady who kept regular hours despite the protracted work stoppage. She had a challenging job since there were no beautifully furnished model homes to show prospective buyers and she had run out of reasons to explain the lack of any construction activity. As far as Romeo knew Lars Jensen still had a place in Haria and could presumably be summoned to the office for a meeting. As they approached Arrecife, Romeo offered to drive them the 30 miles from the airport to Haria and drop them at their hotel. Jake thanked him for the generous offer but thought he had better rent a car so that they would be free to explore the area. On disembarking, they exchanged hugs and phone numbers and agreed to stay in touch.

After over 20 hours of travel Jake and Laurie were happy to collapse in bed at Finca La Crucita where they had booked a room. With their bodies having no idea what time it was they arose early and after a relaxing breakfast featuring local food and lots of delicious home-grown coffee Jake set off for Haria Valley Homes. Jake had considered and rejected the idea of taking Laurie and posing as prospective buyers. After all, he was a lawyer who had traveled a great distance on behalf of his client to confront Lars Jensen and this was no time to play games. The sales office was, as advertised by Romeo, a charming small version of a home. The exterior was a brilliant white with beautiful green frames around every window as well as the front door. This was a trademark Cesar Manrique look that dominated the homes as well as the commercial buildings in Haria. Although it sounds like it could be boring and monotonous it somehow worked exceedingly well in Haria as well as in other areas in Lanzarote. The building was no more than 800 square feet comprised of a reception area, conference room and restroom. Besides the renderings of the homes the walls were covered with Cesar Manrique paintings. Starting at the airport you couldn't get away from this guy.

Jake entered the building and was greeted by an attractive young woman seated at a reception desk. She introduced herself as Irma as could be seen from the fancy nametag pinned to her jacket. Jake handed her his business card and said he was there representing one of the investors and would like to meet with Mr. Jensen. Irma became visibly nervous – this was clearly not the first time she had heard from an investor but undoubtedly the first time a lawyer had shown up in person. She excused herself and went into the conference room closing the door before calling Lars Jensen. Jake was not surprised that she made the call in private and that she obviously was having a lengthy conversation with Jensen. She emerged from the conference room and advised Jake that Mr. Jensen could meet with him the following morning at 10:00 a.m.

In his light gray expensive suit, white shirt open at the collar, slicked back salt & pepper hair, and pencil thin moustache Lars Jensen exuded confidence. He kept Jake waiting and showed up at 10:15 for their meeting. Jake had a narcissistic client who had read in a book that he last one to arrive at a meeting has the most power – perhaps Lars had read the same book.

In the 24 hours since Irma had called, Lars had clearly anticipated the reason for Jake's visit and was well prepared for the meeting. He blamed the problems experienced on the project on just about everyone but himself. When Jake mentioned an accounting of the money that had been invested by Poul and others Lars pivoted to how the project was going to be saved by the infusion of additional money by a Japanese firm that would become a partner. He hastened to add that the interest to be acquired by the new firm would come from Lar's share of the project and thus would not have an impact on the private investors. Lars produced a summary of the new joint venture which included pro-forma optimistic projections indicating a return of the original investors' money along with substantial profits. When Jake pressed him for more details and copies of any documents regarding the joint venture Lars balked and said the deal was not yet finalized which is the reason he had not yet informed the investors. You didn't have to be an experienced litigator to question the credibility of Lars' story. The meeting ended with Jake telling Lars he would be reporting to his client and be back in touch the next day.

Jake went back to the hotel and luckily Laurie was in the room since she was always a good sounding board. After flinging himself on the bed he asked Laurie to sit by him and after giving her a kiss told her about the meeting and a huge wakeup call he experienced. Sure – he had told Poul they may have to hire an attorney in the Canary Islands but when he boarded the plane for Madrid he was thinking that he could resolve any legal problem anywhere in the world. A charitable view would be that he was cocky and confident, but a more realistic view was that he had gotten a bit full of himself and that he definitely could not go it alone dealing with Lars. He was glad he had saved Romeo's number and immediately gave him a call. Romeo was pleased to hear from him and asked how he could help. After discussion Romeo gave a strong recommendation that Jake contact Enrique and Maria Rodriguez, a husband and wife law firm in Haria who among other things were both very fluent in English. After checking in with Poul in Copenhagen Jake called their number and Maria answered the phone. Jake introduced himself and discussed the purpose of his call. Maria did a quick conflict check to make sure the firm would have no problem being adverse to Lars Jensen and a meeting was scheduled for the following morning.

The Rodriguez law office was in a charming Casitas in front of their home in an upscale Haria neighborhood. The space beautifully combined the comfortable feeling of a home with the efficiency of a full-service office. Jake felt an instant rapport with Enrique and Maria, a handsome couple appearing to be in their mid-forties and on top of their game. They grasped the situation quickly and said they would be happy to work with Jake in representing Poul. Romeo had not steered Jake wrong – they were well qualified in both real estate development and litigation.

Jake had forewarned Poul that he might get a call during his meeting with Enrique and Maria. They got Poul on the phone and arrangements were agreed upon for Enrique and Maria to take the lead with Jake staying involved as the point man between Poul and his new colleagues. Jake called Irma at Haria Valley Homes to inform her that he would not be calling Lars but that Lars would be hearing from "someone" soon intentionally sounding a bit mysterious. The three attorneys poured over the PPM and Jake brought Enrique and Maria up to speed about the alleged impending new joint venture that was going to save the day.

⇒⊢⊣⇐

Given the fact that the matter had been largely turned over to Enrique and Maria, there was no need to stay any longer in Lanzarote. After a memorable dinner with their new friends, Jake and Laurie planned their trip home. Figuring that they may never be as close to North Africa again they opted for a layover in Morocco with a visit to Marrakesh. They checked into the hotel La Mamounia which had a colorful history including being a favorite of Winston Churchill. Although only in Morocco for a day and a night they were able to experience this totally unique culture visiting a marketplace replete with Souks where sure enough bargaining took place reminiscent of Ingrid Bergman's purchase of a scarf in Casablanca. Jake made a quick trip on his own to the Jemaa el-Fnaa, a wonderful public square with a long colorful history and still featuring, among other things, jugglers and snake charmers. The taxi taking him there was filled with hashish smoke giving him a pleasant contact high. Their Canary Islands/Morocco adventure having ended, Jake and Laurie headed home to Santa Monica.

COLLEEN ROBBINS

On a Monday morning while sitting in his office in Marina Del Rey Jake received a call.

"My name is Colleen Robbins and I would like to make an appointment to see you a soon as possible."

" I would be happy to see you—how did you happen to call me?"

"There's a story behind that and I would rather explain in person"

Jake, intrigued, made arrangments for Colleen to come in at 9:30 the next morning.

Arriving promptly on schedule Colleen was attractive in a very special way. About 5'7" tall she had gorgeous brown hair down to her shoulders. It had blond highlights that were not from a beauty salon but from nature like a fine piece of mahagony. She was smartly dressed with a nice figure and no overly exposed flesh. Jake guessed Colleen to be in her late forties perhaps a well preserved early fifties. Her most striking feature which almost knocked Jake out of his chair was her eyes—big, brown and beautifully expressive revealing both high intelligence and severe pain.

"You mentioned you were going to tell me how you happened to call me"

"It's no big deal but a bit embarrasing. You don't know me, at least not yet, but I am not in the habit of going to bars particularly alone. Last week I happened to stop by the Café Swiss on Rodeo Drive in Beverly Hills and took a seat at the bar. In the middle of my third glass of wine I began to spill my guts to the bartender—that's the embarrasing part—like a cliché in a movie—using a bartender as a confessional. I guess I had to share my frustration with somone about the dreadful outcome of my recent divorce. I told him how I felt my lawyer and I were outsmarted by my husband and his lawyer and let them get away with murder. I asked the bartender if he knew of a good attorney who could take on a tough case and he mentioned you."

"Was his name Henry by any chance."

"It was Henry all right—he said you used to come in several times a week with your law partner—a guy named Bill and that Bill had tragically died young and he hadn't seen you since but heard through the grapevine that you had become a tenacious lawyer who liked detective work as much if not more than legal work". Jake felt flattered that he had actualy developed a reputation in Beverly Hills of all places.

"Henry would have no way of knowing this but I must tell you I do not specialize in family law. Sure I handled a few divorces years ago but don't currently practice in that field".

"That's not an issue for me—I've been down the family lawyer road. My attorney Murray Rose is a very experienced divorce lawyer but that got me nowhere. What I need is someone who can prove my husband lied in court and managed to hide substantial assets."

The meeting continued for over an hour with Jake asking many questions to try and get a handle on Colleen's relationship with her now ex husband along with any other family dynamics. It turned out that Colleen's ex was Jason Sweeney someone Jake knew of as a prominent commercial developer specializing in high profile office buildings. It became clear to Jake that Jason was a full blown narcissist with a sociopathic twist. His devastation of the marrage was not very original. Panicking about turning sixty he took up with a youger woman an administrative assistant in her mid twenties. Her name even a sounded like a bimbo—Tammy for Christ's sake. Jason was either very careless or had an unconcious wish to be caught. He had even left a copy of a receipt on his dresser for a room at a Santa Monica hotel in mid-week (perhaps an afternoon).

Jake asked about children and Colleen's answers were interesting and instructive. There were two adult children whose paths had gone in a rather counter intuitive ways based on their genders and in the son's case even his name. He was Jason, Jr. but had distanced himself from his father to the point of not even using the name Jason but rather going by his middle name Lynn. He had no interest in his father's business and was happy living in a modest apartment and teaching English in a high school in Pasadena. He was very loyal to Colleen and made it a point to visit her at least once a week. The daughter Cheryl had gone the other way—a daddy's girl from day one and a budding narcissist in her own right. In a horrible slap in the face to Colleen she even hung out with Tammy knowing of the affair with her father.

Jake asked Colleen the basis for her belief that Jason had lied and withheld critical information regarding the nature, extent and whereabouts of his assets. If there was solid proof presumably her attorney Maury Rose would have presented it in court. Colleen conceded that of course she had no proof but believed that Maury had failed to follow up on some potential leads.

"Do you happen to have a copy of the transcript of Jason's pre-trial depostion" Jake inquired.

"I do and it's about 400 pages long—the deposition lasted for two full days."

It was agreed that Colleen would deliver the transcript to Jake and they would meet again after his review and among other things discuss whether or not Jake would be retained. Colleen wasted no time and early the next morning she delivered the transcript to Jake's office. Reading a deposition taken by another attorney had a voyouristic feel about it combined with some serious Monday morning quarterbacking. Every attorney has a distinct style in questioning witnesses. The Sina Qua Non of effective cross examination is tenacious follow up when it becomes clear that the witness is not being forthcoming. On cross examination of a hostile witness it is perfectly proper to ask "Isn't it true" type leading questions. It was clear that Maury's follow up in his examination of Jason was lacking.

The singular most important line of questioning Jake came across involved a discussion of a man named Charles

Abbott. He was someone who had invested $3,000,000 in Jason's most recent project, a high-rise office building in the mid-Wilshire section of Los Angeles and had apparantly lost it all. Jake immediately called Colleen and asked if Maury had taken the deposition of Charles Abbott and was shocked to see that the answer was no. It was time for a heart to heart chat with Colleen. He invited her to lunch and expressed his interest in handling her case.

"If it can be established that Jason either perjured himself or committed fraud the remedy would be to reopen the divorce case and I assume Maury is still your attorney of record. I don't believe any useful purpose would be served by aggressively firing him as it is too soon to know how much damage has been done and besides it would be beneficial to keep him as an ally and not alienate him. How would you feel about my contacting him and candidly disussing your concerns. He will of course know he is being second guessed but under the circumstance would probably welcome a friendly transition of the case."

"That's fine with me. I have nothing against Maury and just want to find out if I have been screwed by Jason. God knows he hasn't screwed me in the other sense in a long time."

Jake admired Colleen's sense of humor under the circumstances and could see the genuine pain in her eyes. He really wanted to help this woman.

The meeting with Maury went remarkably well. He was a good guy and felt horrible about the outcome of the case and welcomed Jake's involvement. They agreed that Jake would take over the representation of Colleen for the purpose of conducting an investigation but to defer a formal substitution of attorneys with the court until it was detemined that there was a solid ground for re-opening the case. No sense tipping off Jason and his lawyer that they may not have heard the last from Colleen.

Jake left the meeting feeling very good—he was now free to do what he liked best –detective work. He had no trouble finding a telephone number for Charles Abbott. When he introduced himself as Colleen's attorney and told him he would like to talk to him about Jason Robbins, Charles was receptive and appeared to be anxious to meet. Jake suggested lunch at Café Swiss the next day—it somehow seemed appropriate to finally venture back to the scene of so many long lunches with Bill Fitzgerald and besides he wanted to thank Henry for referring Colleen to him. Jake was sitting at the bar reuniting with Henry when he spotted a man approach the hostess stand and he knew he must be Abbott. Tall, impeccably dressed, gray hair, about mid 60ish he looked like a guy who could afford to lose millions. He strolled over to the hostess stand.

"Are you Mr. Abbott?"

"I am but please make it Charles. You must be Jake."

The hostess escorted them to a quiet booth towards the rear of the restaurant.

Charles had either done some research about Jake or was very perceptive—probably both. He assumed the purpose of the meeting was to "dig up some dirt" about Jason Robbins. Nothing unites people better than a common enemy. After exchanging pleasantries Jake began.

"I understand how it might be painful to talk about losing $3,000,000 but I am hoping your story can lead to some useful information that could be helpful to my client."

"Don't worry about my feelings. I'm a big boy and I wouldn't have invested money I couldn't afford to lose. I will tell you the story even though it is in some respects very embarrassing".

Charles went on to explain how he had made his money investing in start ups in Silicon Valley. A few years ago he was introduced to a man named Terrence Johnston who described himself as a broker but one who instead of arranging loans arranged for investments of equity. His pitch was that investors didn't just get interest from making loans but rather received partial ownership of valuable real estate. He said he represented somone named Jason Robbins who had tied up an incredible site in the mid-Wilshre section of Los Angeles one of the last available for a mid to highrise office building along the valuable Miracle Mile corridor. A Letter of Intent had been entered into with United Life Insurance (ULI) one of the many life insurance companies financing high profile office buildings at the time.

The proposed deal had a unique structure. Of the projected costs of $30,000,000 ULI would put up $27,000,000 but wanted their co-developer partner to have 10% or $3,000,000 of "skin in the game". For heading up the development the partner, in this case Jason's company— Robbins Development, would receive a 50% interest in the project. Jason was a very clever fellow—his Modus Operandi was to tie up good sites, hire architects and others to design the project and obtain the necessary approvals and then use other people's money to finance the development. To satisfy ULI's "skin in the game" requirement his plan was to use other people's "skin" in this case it turned out to be Charles.

Charles went on but Jake could tell he was reaching the painful part. First of all why would someone who had made a fortune in computer and internet related businesses suddenly go into real estate where he had virtually no expertise? Charles explained that his Silicon Valley investments all seemed so intangible—software and technology that you couldn't touch and feel. He felt that owning a piece of a beautiful and successful building would be a welcome contrast to a bunch of shares of stock. Terrence had picqued his ineterest enough to agree to a meeting with Jason.

When meeting a potential, investor Jason was on his most charming and persuasive best behavior. He was exteremely well prepared with tremendous visual materials comprised of renderings, elevations and floor plans along with very optimistic financial projections. He boasted that by having the ULI money invested as equity rather than debt it could not be foreclosed in the event of unforseen problems. What he failed to explain and this is where Charles failed miserably in his due diligence was that the deal with ULI had a remedy that was actually worse than foreclosure. There was a provision for capital calls (50% from each partner) to cover any cost over-runs coupled with an equity squeeze down clause that provided that in the event one partner failed to come up with their share their ownership interest would be reduced in accordance with a very aggressive formula. This was hardly mentioned and glossed over with the notion that the budget had a large cushion to cover unanticipated costs.

A second meeting was scheduled and the architect and contractor were introduced to Charles and made an excellent presentation regarding both the design features and the construction issues. Jason went into a closing mode and concluded a deal with Charles whereby Charles would share 50/50 Jason's 50% interest in the project. In short Charles for $3,000,000 would end up with a 25% interest in a $30,000,000 project with tremendous upside potential a sweet deal he couldn't turn down. With the commitment from Charles in his hip pocket Jason was able to finalize the transaction with ULI.

The project encountered substantial over-runs on day one. The site had been occupied by a two story building with a restaurant on the ground floor which had been built many years before both lead paint and asbestos became illegal. Despite his experience Jason's due diligence was lacking and failed to take into account the very substantial costs of demolishing a building containing toxic materials. In addition during excavation costs went way above the estimated amount (sounded all too familiar to Jake). Other extra costs had to be added to meet the competition along Wilshire Boulevard in terms of materials and amenities - so much for Jake the genious developer. Additional cost overruns were encountered throughout the development of the project. Colleen wondered to herself whether Jason's lack of his usual attention to detail was attributable to distractions related to his dalliance with Tammy.

ULI made a capital call demand and easily put up it's one half share Jason always on the ragged edge of available cash turned to Charles to put up their share. Charles made a decision not to invest more money which resulted in the first of a series of equity squeeze downs which effectively transferred the lion's share of ownership to ULI.

From reviewing Charles' deposition Jake already knew that the devestating loss on the mid-Wilshire project was one of the primary reasons for the court's decision that the amount of community property to be divided was very limited. Jason indeed owned other properties but they were all highly leveraged and thus had limited equity.

Jake's hope in meeting with Charles was to perhaps get a clue as to any hidden assets which were withheld from consideration by the court. Charles was very astute and had surmised what Jake was looking for and his willingness and in fact eagerness to cooperate was the satisfaction of somehow getting back at Jason for taking advanatge of him.

Without being asked he volunteered that during the course of his involvement in the mid-Wilshire project he had naturally spent a lot of time with Jason who especially after a few cocktails would brag about how he cleverly and strategically hired the best available specialists to advise him on various aspects of his business. He mentioned a Santa Monica attorney highly specialtized in asset protection.

"Asset Protection" is a perfetly legitimate concept in a number of contexts including safety and tax savings but can also be a euphanism for hiding assets from creditors or as Jake suspected in this case from soon to be ex-wives. Jake had learned that is always a "place du jour" best know for stashing money outside of the United States which in his memory had included Switzerland, Lichtenstein, Bermuda, The Caymans, The Bahamas, Cook Islands and The Ilse of Man.

After meeting with Charles Jake was very happy about the way he and Colleen had handled Maury Rose. Although not a family law specialist Jake knew enough to realize that you can't re-open a divorce case on a mere suspicion that one of the parties had withheld important iformation at the time of trial. You couldn't say in effect "Hey I think the husband may have had hidden assets off shore." You would have to have some solid evidence to re-open and it was time for a candid conversation with Maury Rose.

Jake called Maury and set up a breakfast meeting at Nat N Al's in Beverly Hills a bit of a cliché for a place to meet a jewish lawyer but oh well. He brought Maury up to date on his meeting with Charles Abbott and they brainstormed as to what would be needed to re-open the case. It was refreshing for Jake who had become somewhat of a pathological lone wolf to be actually collaberating with another lawyer. Maury came up with an interesting idea—look up asset protection lawyers in Santa Monica—couldn't be too many—and contact them for a consulta-tion about safe places to place money abroad. It didn't take long to identify Kevin Long a Santa Monica lawyer who advertized quite extensively about his specialization in asset protection.

Although Jake couldn't be sure if Kevin Long had actu-ally represented Jason he went to his Website to see what he could learn. Sure enough Kevin Long was highly special-ized in asset proetction and his Website was a treasure trove of valuable information. It turns out that the IRS with the help of Congress had become quite pro-active in preventing or discovering various tax avoidance schemes. Switzerland's bank secrecy laws had been pretty much eviserated and thus Swiss bank accounts were somewhat passe. Jake learned from Kevin's Website that asset protection involved a com-bination of setting up entities that hid the identity of the underlying owner and having these entities established in certain favored off shore locations.

The most common structure is an Offshore Asset Protection Trust (OAPT) which removes assets placed in the trust from the jurisdition of United States courts. As a further layer of protection/secrecy the OAPT is established by a separate legal entity such as a Limited Liability Company or a Corporation. The individual behind the underlying entity gets the best of both worlds—protection and as much secrecy as possible.

Now Jake's task was to connect enough dots to persuade the divorce court to re-open Colleen's case. Jake had become a twice a day meditator which he had discovered was very good for stress management and would sometimes open his mind to something he might not have otherwise considered. He came out of a mid-afternoon meditation and an idea hit him over the head making him wonder why he hadn't thought of it sooner.

What if Charles Abbott sued Jason claiming assets were hidden from him which if made known could have prevented or at least mitigated the equity squeeze down that had occurred on the Mid-Wilshire? A deposition of Jason in a case filed by Charles could lead to evidence that could be used to re-open the divorce. It is unethical for attorneys to solicit business in a way that "stirs up litigation". This is why ambulance chasing is illegal. Sometimes it's better to be lucky than smart and wouldn't you know it—Charles called Jake to request another meeting.

"After our meeting at Café Swiss I got to thinking."

Charles was in Jake's office the morning after their phone converstaion.

" I accepted my $3,000,000 loss without really challanging Jason on his claimed inability to contribute to the capital call to cover the cost over-runs."

Jake in anticipation of the meeting had carefuly connsidered the conflict of interest in representing both Charles and Colleen against Jason. Wouldn't they be competing for the same assets if any were identified? He concluded that the two of them would not only have to waive the conflict but enter into a written agreement as to how to proceed including the division of any money collected from Jason.

It was time for Charles and Colleen to meet. Why not Café Swiss again—it was becoming a part of the whole saga. Jake was not surprised that Charles and Colleen immediately bonded—again the common enemy syndrome. Jake explained the conflict issue and insisted that they reach an agreement with each one of them using independent counsel. An agreement between them came together quite quickly evidencing their eargerness to join forces against Jason.

With the agreement in hand Jake filed a complaint on behalf of Charles Abott against Jason Robbins in the Los Angels County Superior Court in Santa Monica. The complaint alleged fraud based on a misreprentation that Jason did not have the ability to meet the capital calls on the mid-Wilshire project when he in fact did have available cash. The allegations were on "information and belief" which is legal pleading technique which allows a claimant to make allegations without personal knowledge of the facts but at least having a good faith belief that they are true. Charles' "information" was based on Jason's statement about having an asset protection attorney and Jake realized there could be a huge battle with Jason's attorneys as to whether he coud avoid a dismissal and get the case far enough to allow him to take Jason's deposition.

Jake made it past a series of preliminary motions and finally was able to schedule Jason's deposition. This was no small accomplishment—to no one's surprise Jason had retained Nathan Pruitt a prominent and powerful Beverly Hills attorney who was affiliated with the same firm that had represented Jason in the divorce proceedings. Jake knew of Nathan by reputation and he was clearly no slouch and a very worthy adversary.

In most cases before the deposition is taken of an important witness and particularly when it is the other party to the lawsuit a Notice to Produce is served before the deposition to obtain relevant documents in the possesion of the party to be used during the questioning. Jake made an unusual strategic decision to skip the Notice to Produce at least initially and go straight to the deposition. His rationale was to preserve the element of surprise as much as possible and perhaps trip Jason up by getting testimony which could later be impeached by documents subpoened later. This was perhaps a naïve hope with an attorney as good as Nathan on the other side.

After the normal preliminary procedures of having the witness sworn in by the court reporter and giving an appropriate admonition and explanation even though Jake was quite certain that this was not Jason's first deposition the substantive questioning began.

Jake started off by giving Jason the broadest possible definition of what he meant when he asked about "entities" and that it would include any possible organization, company, partnership, LLC, trust or any other type of structure and any possible role played by Jason. He didn't want Jason to at a later date say; "Well—you didn't ask me if I was a beneficiary" or some other lame justification for withholding information.

Jake laboriously took Jason though his many business involvments, past and present. Many of them had already been identified in the divorce proceedings. Real estate developers often form a separate entity for each project for liability, tax and other reasons. Jake had saved the best for last.

"Have you ever been involved directly or indirectly in an Offshore Asset Protection Trust?"

"May I confer with my attorney"

"Of course"

Jason might have put up a billboard that said: "I don't want to answer this question"

While Jason and Nathan were out of the room Jake speculated that Jason was asking whether there was some kind of privilege to withhold information about an OAPT as a part of the secrecy aspect of setting up such an entity. Nathan was an excellent advocate but also a good attorney and he had to break the news to Jason that there was no such "privilege" and he would have to answer.

Forty five minutes later Jake had extracted substantial details about an OAPT which had been formed in The Isle of Man by a Limited Liability Company which in turn had been formed in The Cook Islands and that Jason was the Managing Member of the LLC which is the equivalant of a CEO of a corporation. The Isle of Man Entity was called Santorini, LLC and the Cook Islands entity was Mykonos,

LLC. Jason was obviously a big fan of Greek Islands and islands in general.

When the questioning turned to the holdings of the OAPT Jason instead of trying to rely on a non-existent privilege pleaded ignorance. He acted as though the OAPT was a blind trust whereby he was isolated from any knowledge about the holdings. Although true blind trusts do exist for people holding public office they are virtually non-existent in the private sector.

The deposition came to a quick end with Jason continuing to stonewall Jake as to any details regarding the OAPT. The next step in litigation where a witness stonewalls the attorney taking the deposition without legal justification is a motion in court to compel the witness to answer creating a situation, if the motion is granted, where a continued refusal to answer will put the witness in contempt of court—not a minor offense.

Where an impasse such as this occurs there is always an issue as to who blinks first and sure enough Nathan called Jake to tell him a motion would not be needed and that they could schedule a resumption of the deposition. Jake had learned that when something like this occurs it is counter productive to "gloat" but better to resume the deposition respectfully as though there had been an agreed upon postponement.

Jake began to second guess his earlier decision not to issue a Notice Produce prior to the deposition. He considered postponing the resumption of the deposition to allow time to demand all of the books and records of Santorini, LLC and Mykonos, LLC, but decided to avoid a lengthy delay he would see what he could learn from Jason with the idea that a notice to Produce or Subpoena could come later. Most narcissists are very good liars but Jason lacked prevarication skills and his continued "ignorance" about the affairs and assets of his island hideaways was patently obvious. His lies were primarily of ommssion when he repeatedly said "I don't remember" or "I can't recall" in response to Jake's questioning. The "faulty" memory of the successful and clearly smart Jason Robbins was hard to swallow.

Fast forward—six months later. Jake ultimately obtained copies of the books and records of both off-shore entities and with the help of some forensic accounating experts was able to identify approximately $3,000,000 in previously undisclosed assets. This enabled him to negotiate confidential favorable settlements for both Colleen and Charles who by then had bonded and become friends so that there was no threat of a dispute between them in dividing up the spoils that had been uncovered.

A factor that facilitated the settlements was Jason's fear of public humiliation which is the most devastating thing that can happen to a narcissist.

HOORAY FOR HOLLYWOOD

L ooking back Jake was happy that for the first several years of his law practice there was no Internet and were no smart phones. The result was that people interacted more with each other rather than staring at the screens on their devices. During that era Jake had a habit of frequenting the most popular L.A. watering holes where he had memorable encounters with some interesting and often well-known personalities. These places had colorful histories and unique traditions.

On such spot was Matteo's on Westwood Boulevard a few miles south of UCLA. Dimly lit with leather booths Matteo's was a favorite of Frank Sinatra, Dean Martin, and many other Hollywood notables. There was a gratuitous small model train continuously circling the bar on a track high on the wall just below the ceiling. Unusual décor for a bar but somehow it worked. Jake rarely sat in the main restaurant preferring the bar where you could strike up a conversation with the person seated next to you often some-one interesting and/or well known. Jake was not "star struck" and never asked for an autograph and avoided cliché fawn-ing questions but rather engaged in simple conversations often with memorable results. One evening at Matteo's Jake found himself seated next to Peter Brown who was a law partner of famed Hollywood criminal defense attorney Paul Caruso. They got into a spirited friendly debate about what would be the likely outcome of a pending criminal case involving a famous athlete. Peter challenged Jake to a bet of a "Jackson" over who would be right about the out-come. Not automatically knowing what the hell a "Jackson" was Jake quickly realized it referred to a twenty-dollar bill. He then discovered that there was a long-standing Matteo's tradition that when a bet was made at the bar each party to the bet would give the amount of money bet to Oscar the long-time bartender who would put the cash in a glass and stow it away behind liquor bottles on the shelf. When the outcome of the bet was determined, the winner would come to the bar to collect the money. Jake lost the bet but enjoyed taking part in this colorful ritual.

Another popular spot during that era was the Rangoon Racquet Club on little Santa Monica Boulevard in the heart of Beverly Hills. One evening Jake found himself seated next to David Brown, the husband of Helen Gurley Brown famed editor of Cosmopolitan magazine and author of among other books *Sex and The Single Girl*. David of course was well known in his own right having risen to the position of Executive Vice President of 20th Century Fox working for Darryl F. Zanuck. Jake had a knack for drawing total strang-ers into telling stories which in the case of David Brown were fascinating and revealing to say the least. Talking to such folks had become one of Jake's favorite indoor sports.

An example of approaching people in a different manner than most "fans" was his encounter with Johnny Mathis at a cocktail lounge on the top floor of an office building at the corner of Sunset and Vine (can't get more "Hollywood" than that). Jake was sure that many if not most men that who met Johnny would say something like "The first time I made love with a girl was in the back seat of a car listening to you sing Misty on the radio". Instead, Jake, a track athlete himself, had a wonderful conversation about Johnny's career as a champion high jumper while attending San Francisco State. It was clear that Johnny enjoyed reminiscing about his athletic achievements rather than his singing which had flourished over so many generations.

No remembrance of Hollywood hang outs would be complete without including Musso & Frank Grill on Hollywood Boulevard. Opened in 1919, after 100 years it is still the much the same as it was when it was Charlie Chaplin's favorite eatery. Following in his footsteps were such luminaries as Mary Pickford, Rudolph Valentino, Elizabeth Taylor, Groucho Marx, and Jimmy Stewart to name just a few. There is a booth near the front entrance where Marilyn Monroe insisted as a place to be seen with her husband Joe DiMaggio. The fabled Back Room was a gathering spot for writers including William Faulkner, Raymond Chandler, John Steinbeck, and Aldous Huxley, among others. The food is hearty fare such as steaks and chops – don't go there for kale or quinoa. A menu from the 1920's featured a filet mignon dinner for $1.00! In the drink department their martinis are legendary served at a classic bar adjacent to the rich leather booths. Jake did not go there to hobnob with stars but just to soak up the atmosphere and history which he found invigorating and inspirational.

Jake's fascination with Hollywood was in part attributable to the fact that during his first year of night law school at USC he worked for the Southern California Gas Company as a meter reader and was assigned to their Hollywood office on Ivar Avenue just south of Sunset Boulevard. It was an ideal job since he could usually finish by early afternoon and have several hours to study before attending class. By his second year he had transitioned to Aerospace which was more law related and was helpful years later when he sued various Federal agencies over contract disputes. Nonetheless that first year in Hollywood was truly memorable. He read just about every gas meter in town including up and down Hollywood and Sunset Boulevards as well as the residential areas. In those days, many Hollywood stars lived in the Hollywood Hills (everyone knows the iconic Hollywood sign). This was before many of them migrated westward to Beverly Hills, Santa Monica, and Malibu among other places.

FINAL THOUGHTS

Sometimes profound wisdom can come from unlikely sources including very young children. Jake experienced this one afternoon at Palisades Park which is a lengthy tree lined grassy strip in Santa Monica located on a bluff overlooking the ocean. Jake had just finished a quiet meditation, which had become a regular practice, when he saw 5 children racing around some of the trees in large circles in what appeared to be a game. 4 of them looked to be between 10 and 12 years old while the 5th child was much smaller and younger – around 4. The 4-year-old naturally couldn't keep up with the others and was always lagging far behind.

Jake was tempted to feel sorry for him, but he seemed to accept the fact that when you are 4 that's just the way things are. He paused in front of Jake, they made eye contact, and this exchange took place:

"That looks like an interesting game – what is it?"

Without hesitation the 4-year-old replied: "It's just like Tag except you are always It". Wow thought Jake – how many people feel that they are always It? He knew that he did.

❦

One of Jake's favorite quotes by another attorney came from Brendan Sullivan a prominent Washington D.C. lawyer who represented Lt. Col. Oliver North at a hearing conducted by a House-Senate Joint Committee investigating the Iran Contra scandal. The hearing was chaired by Senator Daniel Inouye who after numerous objections by Sullivan reminded him that the hearing was not being held in a court of law and thus the rules of evidence did not apply and suggested that Sullivan let the witness speak for himself.

Sullivan's reply was: *"Well sir, I'm not a potted plant. I'm here as the lawyer. That's my job."* Jake definitely was not a potted plant.

In reflecting on why he had taken the path he did as a lawyer, Jake thought of his favorite quote from literature which is from Hamlet and is included in the advice Polonius gives to his son Laertes as he was leaving Denmark to attend school in France. After telling him "Neither a borrower nor lender be" and "Give every man thine ear, but few thy voice" (in other words it is better to listen more and talk less), his final advice which resonated with Jake was *"But this above all to thine own self be true"*.